AF255480

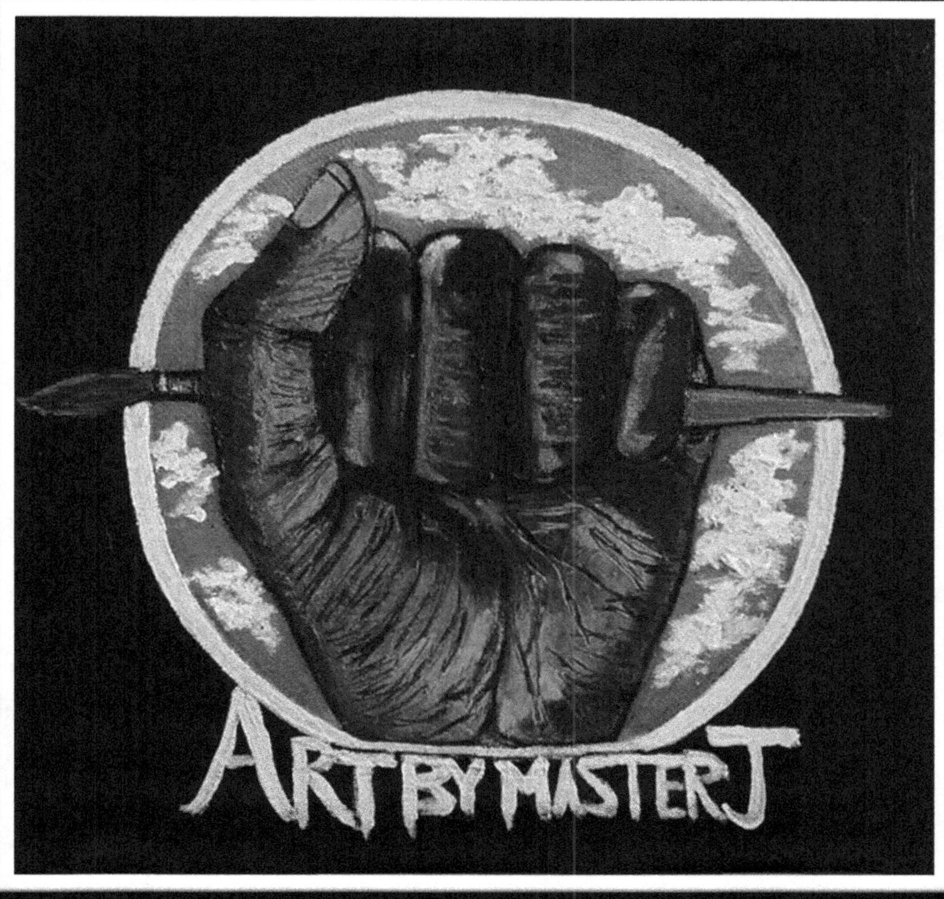

COFFEE TABLE BOOK OF ORIGINAL MASTERPIECES

Cover design: Book Lover Publishing, 2022

Printed in the United States of America

ISBN Hardback 978-1-953473-19-6

ISBN Paperback 978-1-953473-18-9

LCCN: 2022909857

Purple Pearls Publishing, Oceano, California

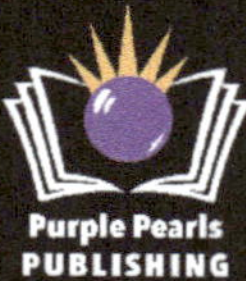

ART BY MASTER J

COFFEE TABLE BOOK OF ORIGINAL MASTERPIECES

For my mom, my sisters,
my love, Shamara,
my friends, and my supporters.

Thank you from the bottom of my heart.

The Divided Soul of Marvin Gaye

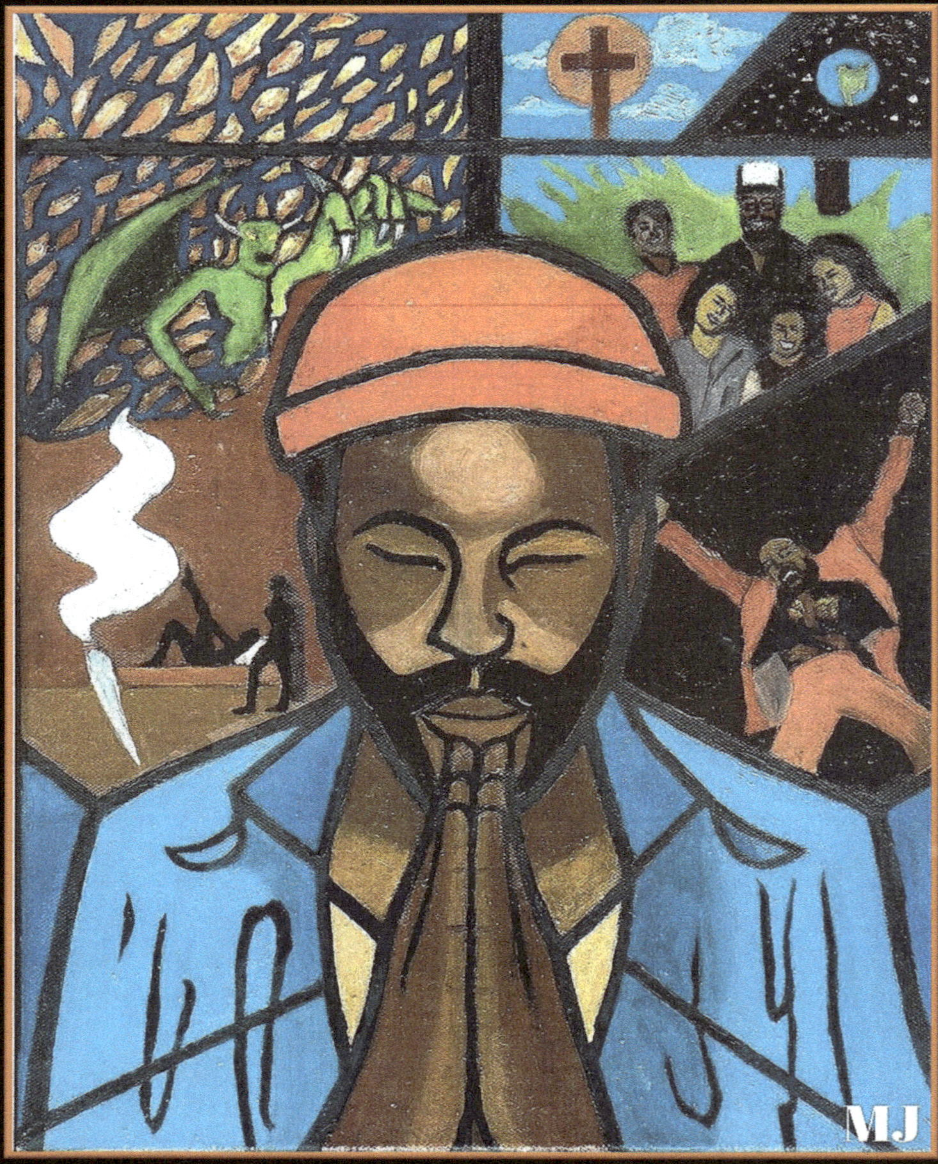

<u>*2006*</u>

Oil on Canvas

This is a portrait that I created of my favorite singer, Marvin Gaye, as an assignment while in college. Around that time, I read a book written by author, Eric Dyson based on the life of Marvin Gaye. The book, which inspired me to paint this portrait, touched on his traumatic childhood, music, the themes behind them, and the demons he struggled with.

I wanted to give the appearance of stained glass like those in a Church to reflect Marvin Gaye's' strong belief in God. The painting shows Marvin Gaye centered in the middle, on his right are the negative things in his life, while on his left are the good things in his life. Marvin is seen in the center praying for inner peace

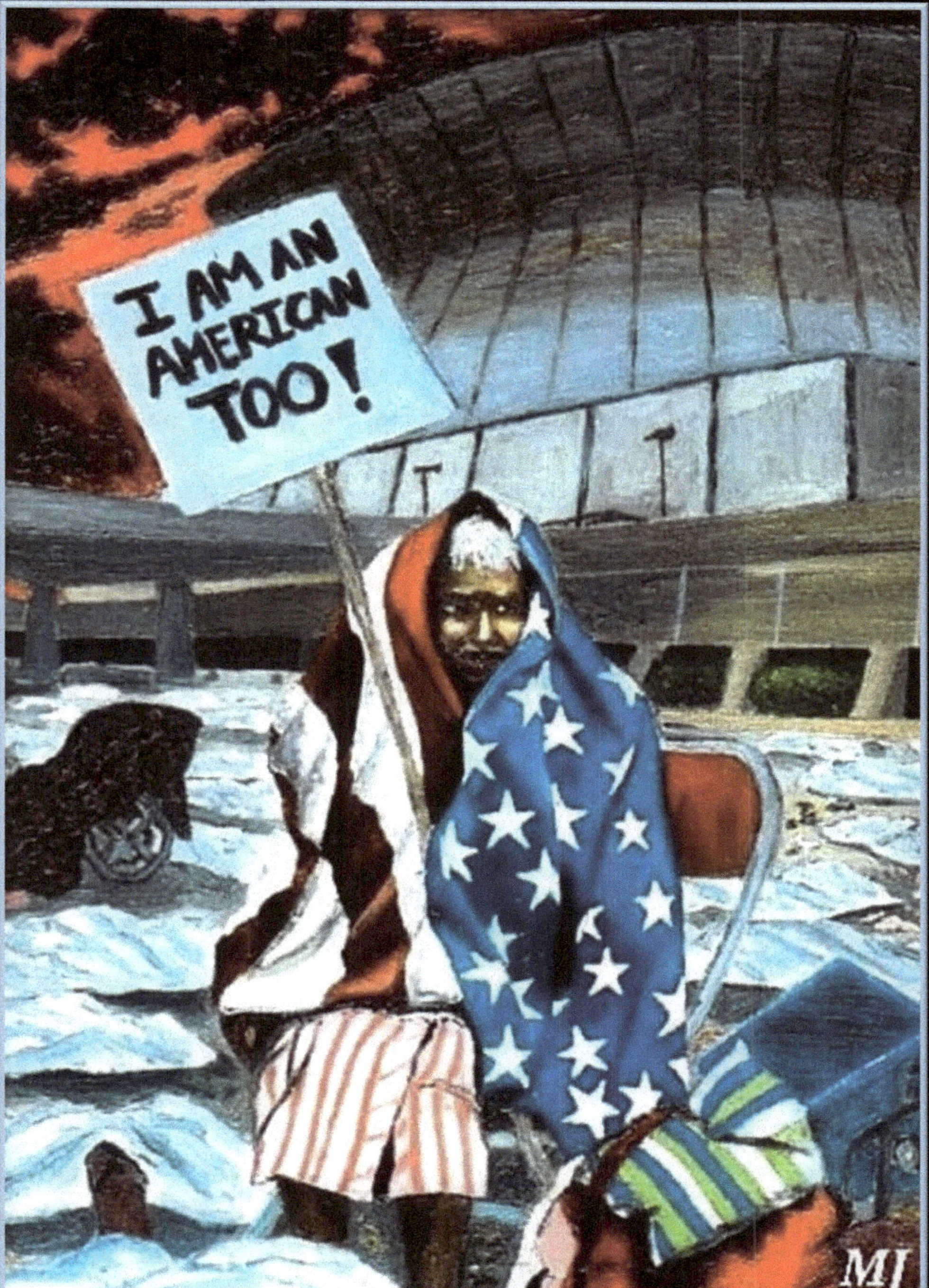

2006
Oil on Canvas

This painting was done with oil paint on canvas. It was created while I was in college as an assignment. I chose to touch on Hurricane Katrina and the devastation that was caused to the city of New Orleans, Louisiana in 2005. Broken levees caused major flooding and help from the Government and FEMA took days to arrive. Hundreds of people died from the major saturation and dehydration. I have family that lives in New Orleans, so this hit home for me, and I felt that it was important for me to express my feelings and thoughts on the situation that occurred.

The painting shows an elderly woman sitting on a chair covered in the American flag holding up a sign that says, I Am an American Too. She is sitting in front of Super Dome stadium and is surrounded by dead bodies of those who didn't survive. The painting is titled, Hell on Earth in New Orleans, to summarize the pain and neglect that the citizens endured during that awful time. The sky was painted red to symbolize the title. Thankfully, the city of New Orleans bounced back, but Hurricane Katrina will never be forgotten.

Brooklyn Benches

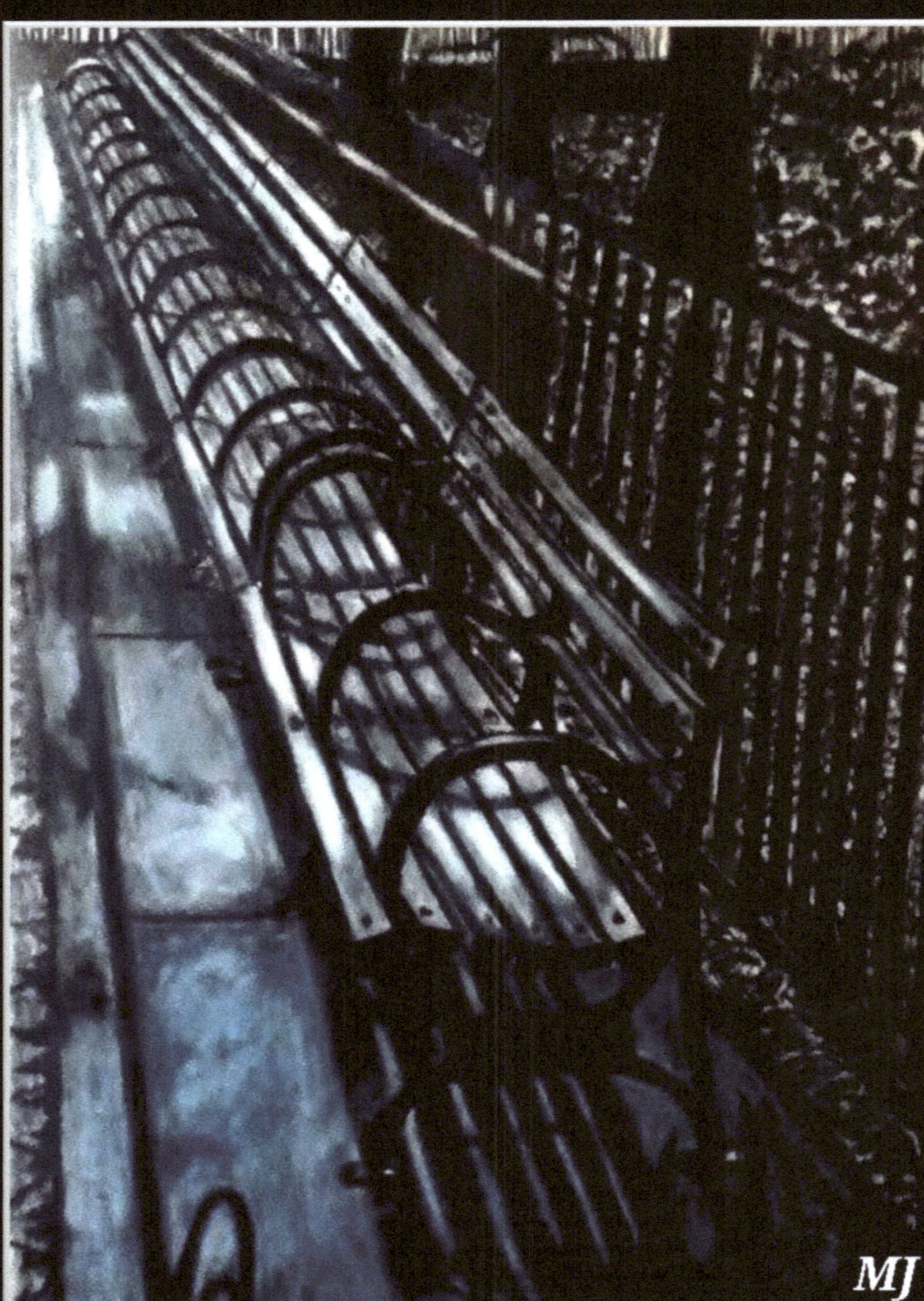

<u>2012</u>
*Graphite on
Paper*

*This drawing was
inspired by an
actual photo that I
took while in
college.*

MJ

Self Portrait

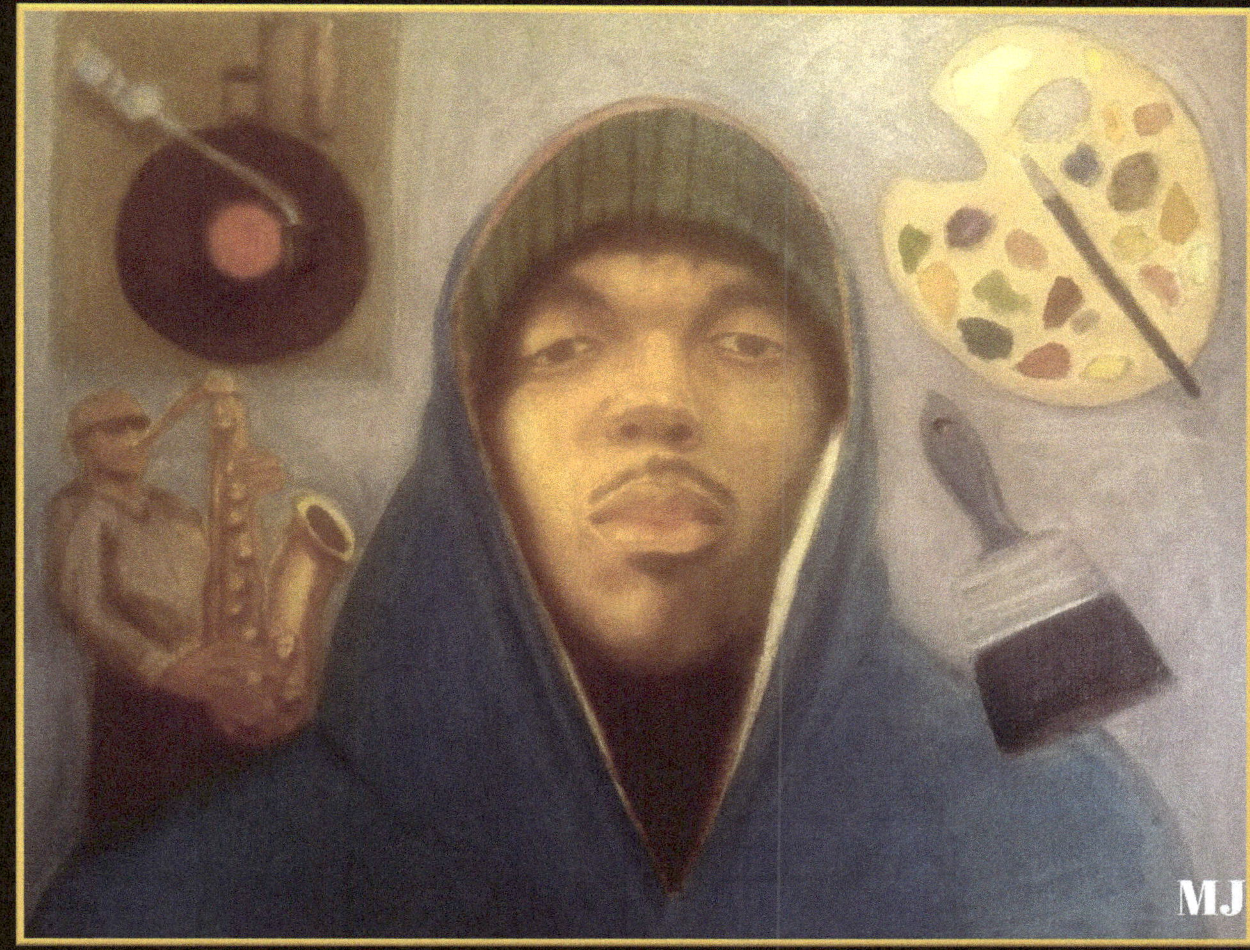

2016
Oil on Canvas

This painting was done in an art class inside a small gallery in Harlem. One important thing I learned about being an artist is that you must remain consistent with the ability to create, or it may leave you. For example, I was painting a lot while in college, but when I finished school and started working a regular job, I eventually stopped painting and stuck with only drawing because I felt that I lacked space for it. Little did I know, my ability to paint started to leave me so I had to teach myself to paint all over again. One of the assignments was to create a self-portrait and include things that helped define who I am. In the painting, I am surrounded by an easel, paint brushes, a record player, and a saxophone player. Showing my love for art and music, and how they play a huge part in who I am.

Dad Can You Help Me Tie a Tie

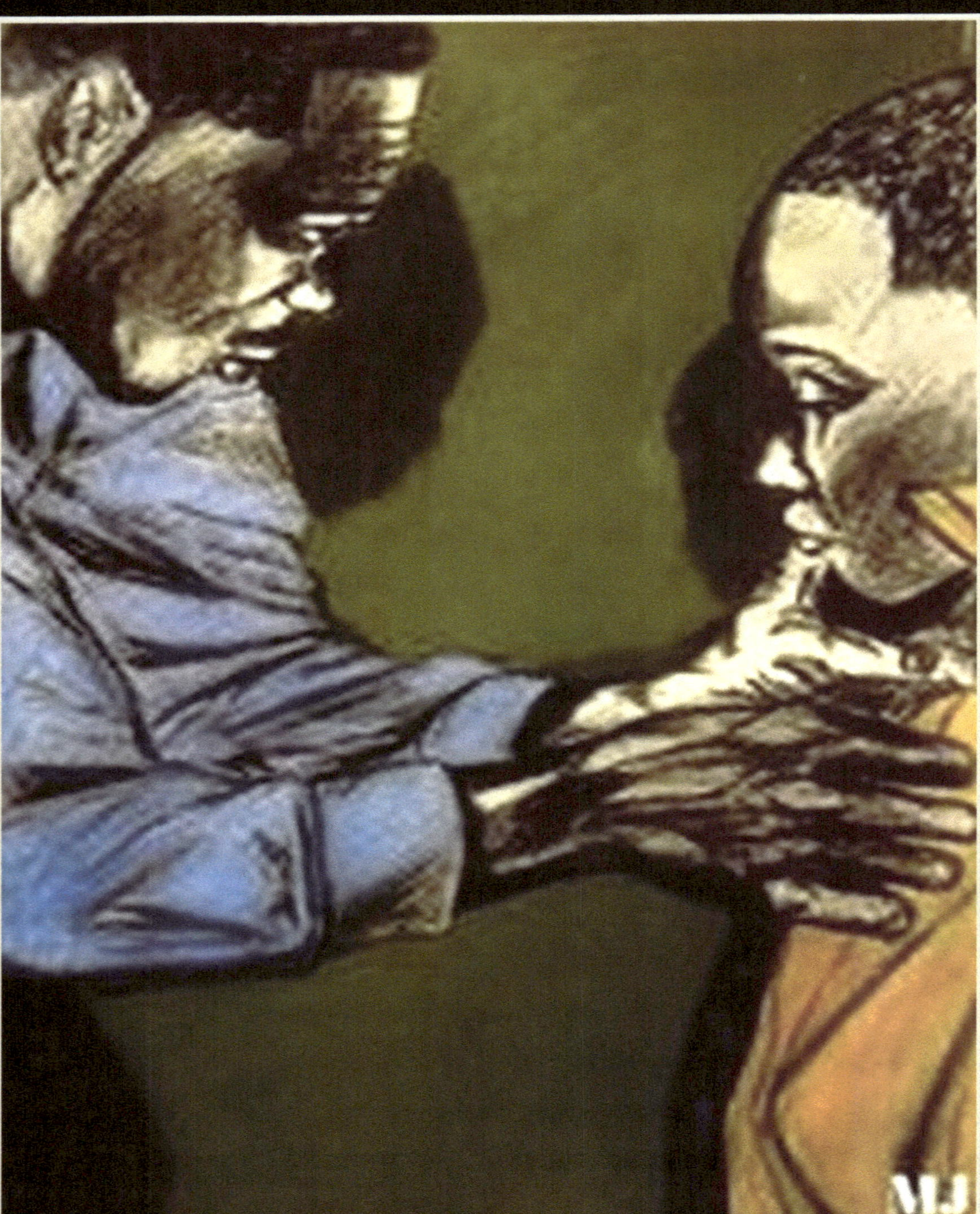

*2016
Colored
pencil on
paper*

This drawing is of a father teaching his son how to tie a tie.

I just wanted to show the importance of father-head and how much it is needed, especially within the black family.

Rooted In Love

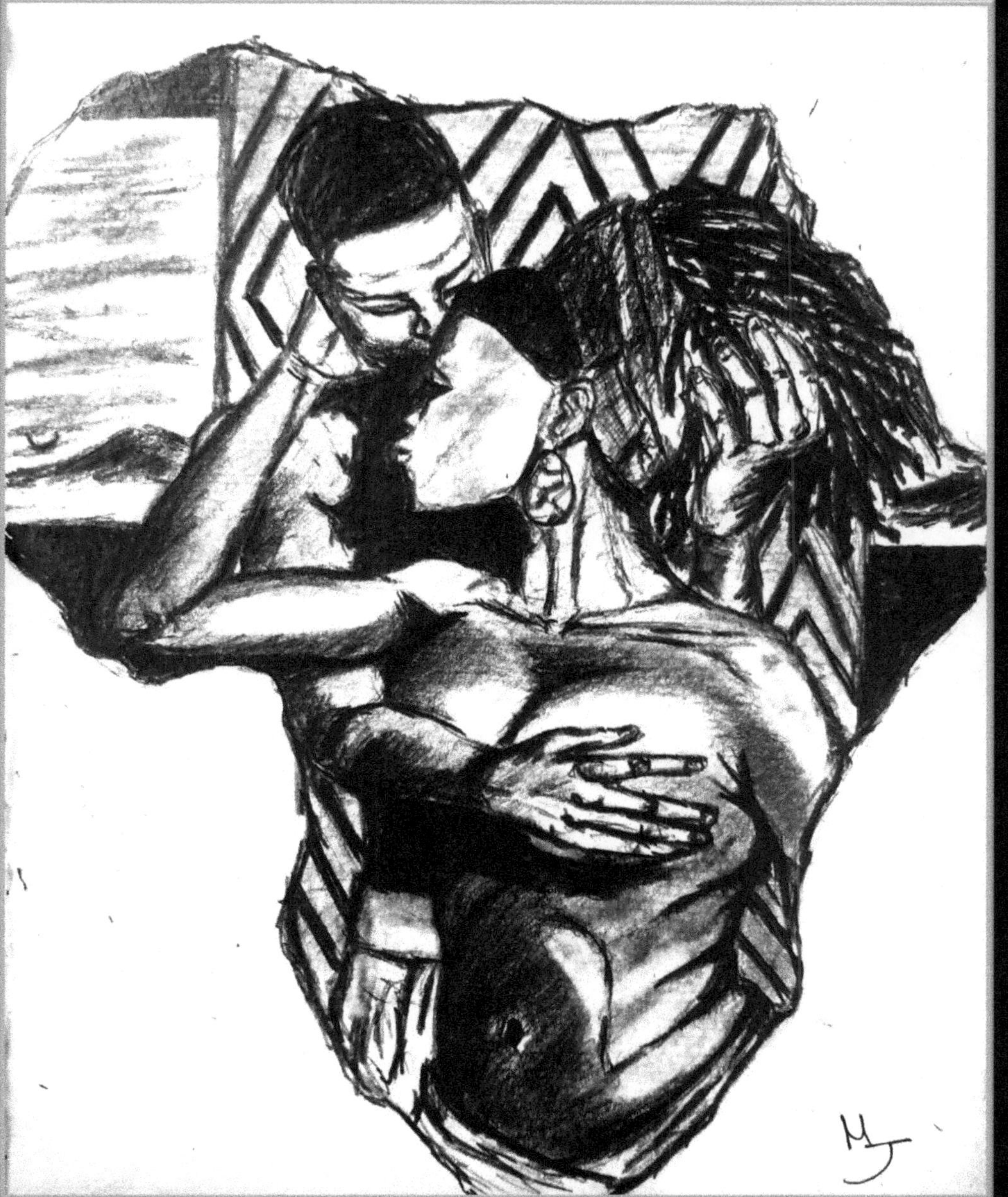

<u>2016</u>
Graphite Pencil on Paper

Around this time, I became heavily involved in creating black love themed artwork. Also, around this time I incorporated the skills that I have learned from art class which helped a lot in making my art appear more realistic.

This drawing is titled, Rooted in Love. It shows a couple together in an embrace, leaning against a column. In the background shows mountains and it is all in the shape of the continent of Africa.

King and Queen

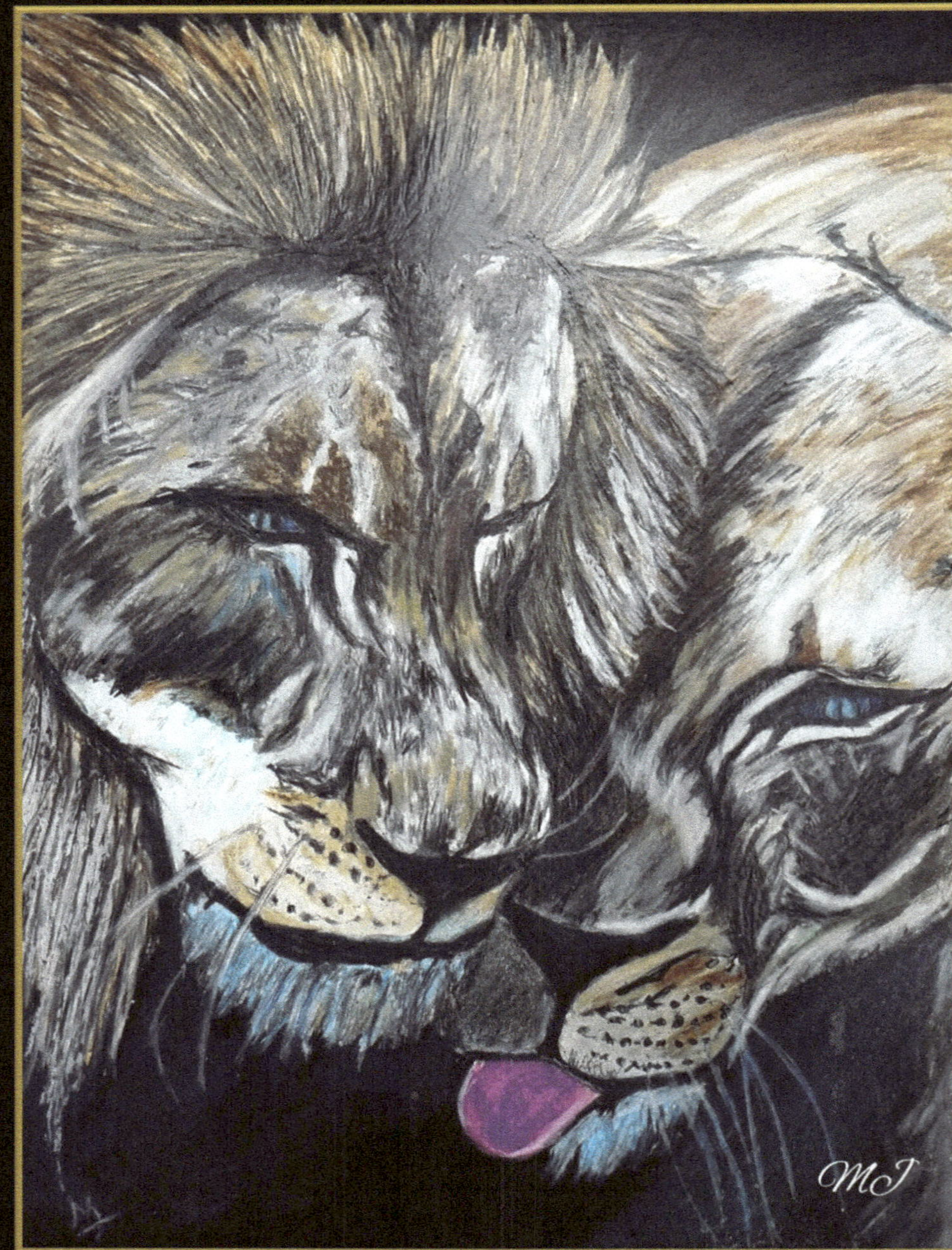

Lions are some of my favorite animals. I admire their ambition and fearlessness. Lions are considered the royalty of animals, so I gave this portrait the name King/Queen.

This drawing shows a lion and lioness hugged together displayed as a couple.

Portrait of Wesley Snipes as Blade

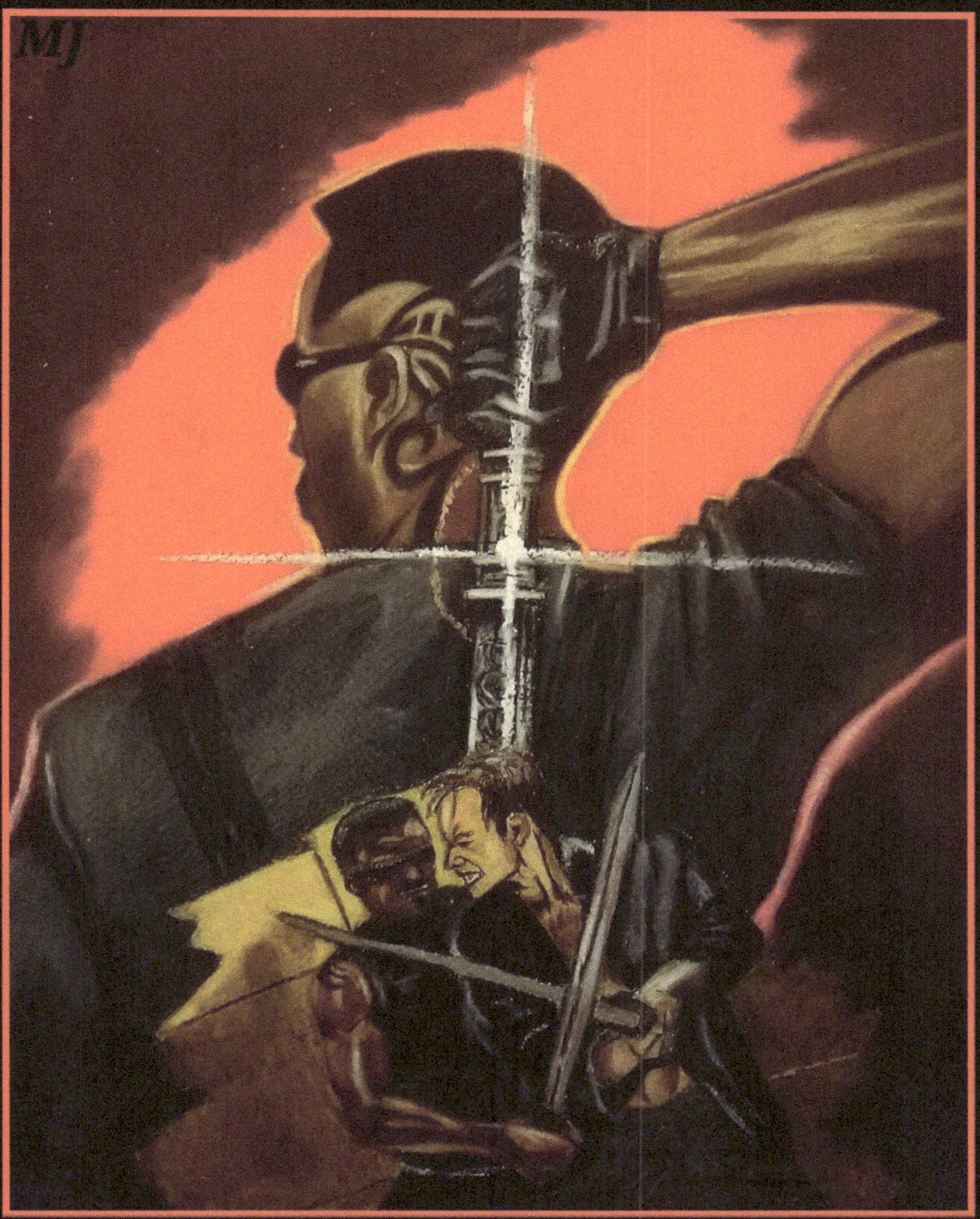

2017
Colored pencils and Oil Pastels

In this portrait, I wanted to pay homage to Wesley Snipes and his performance as Marvel character, Blade. Blade is a half-breed vampire who spends most of his life seeking revenge for the death of his mother and for being born with the vampire curse. He makes it his mission to rid the world of vampires. This portrait is mainly dedicated to the first film from the film trilogy that was created.

It shows Blade holding his sword, while down below shows Blade in sword battle with villain, Deacon Frost.

Nas and His Dad

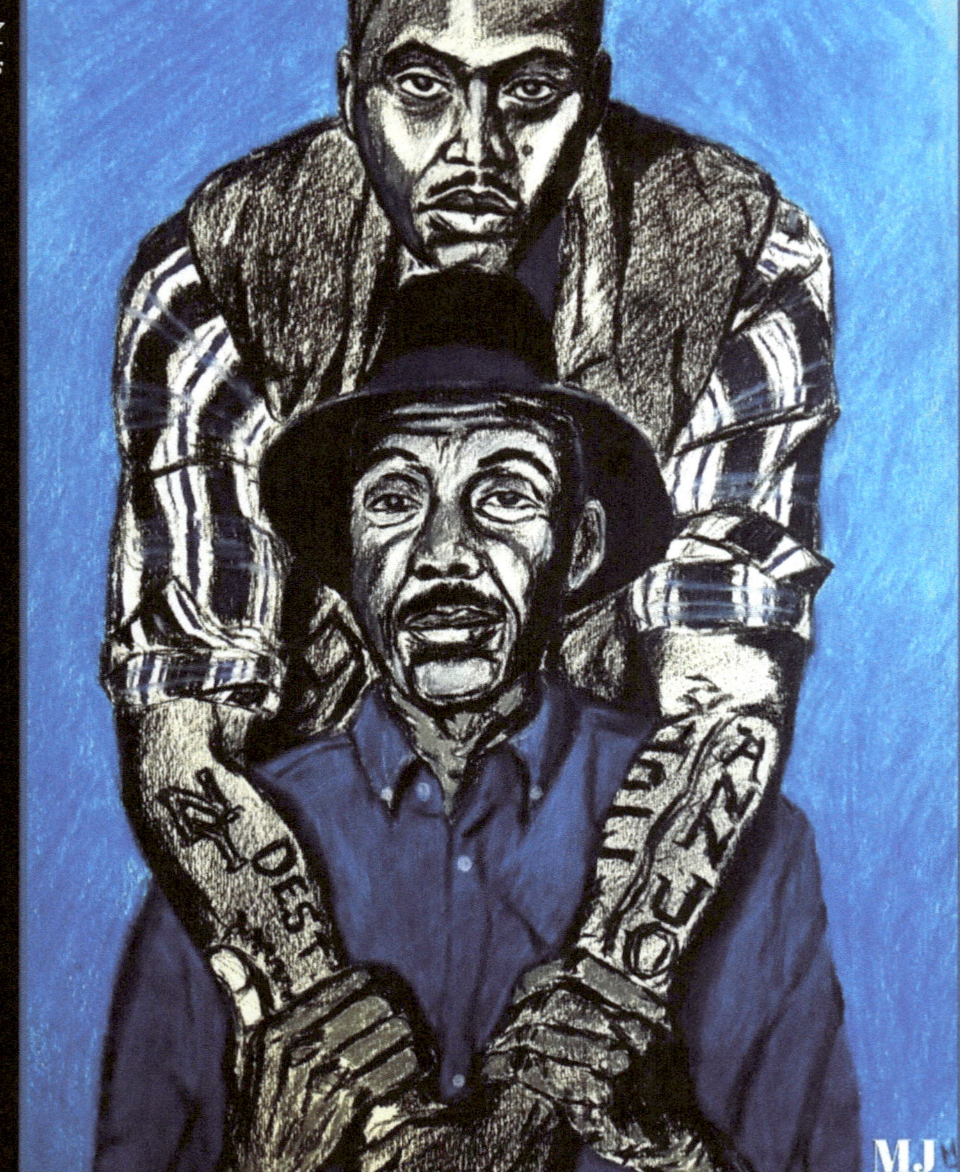

I am a huge fan of Hip Hop artist, Nas. When I drew this portrait of him and his father, Olu Dara Jones, I thought about this song called, *Bridging the Gap*, that they made together.

The portrait was done with only a blue colored pencil and shows Nas holding his father. I wanted to show the tight bond that they have together.

How Can I Ever Leave You, You Always Hold Me Down

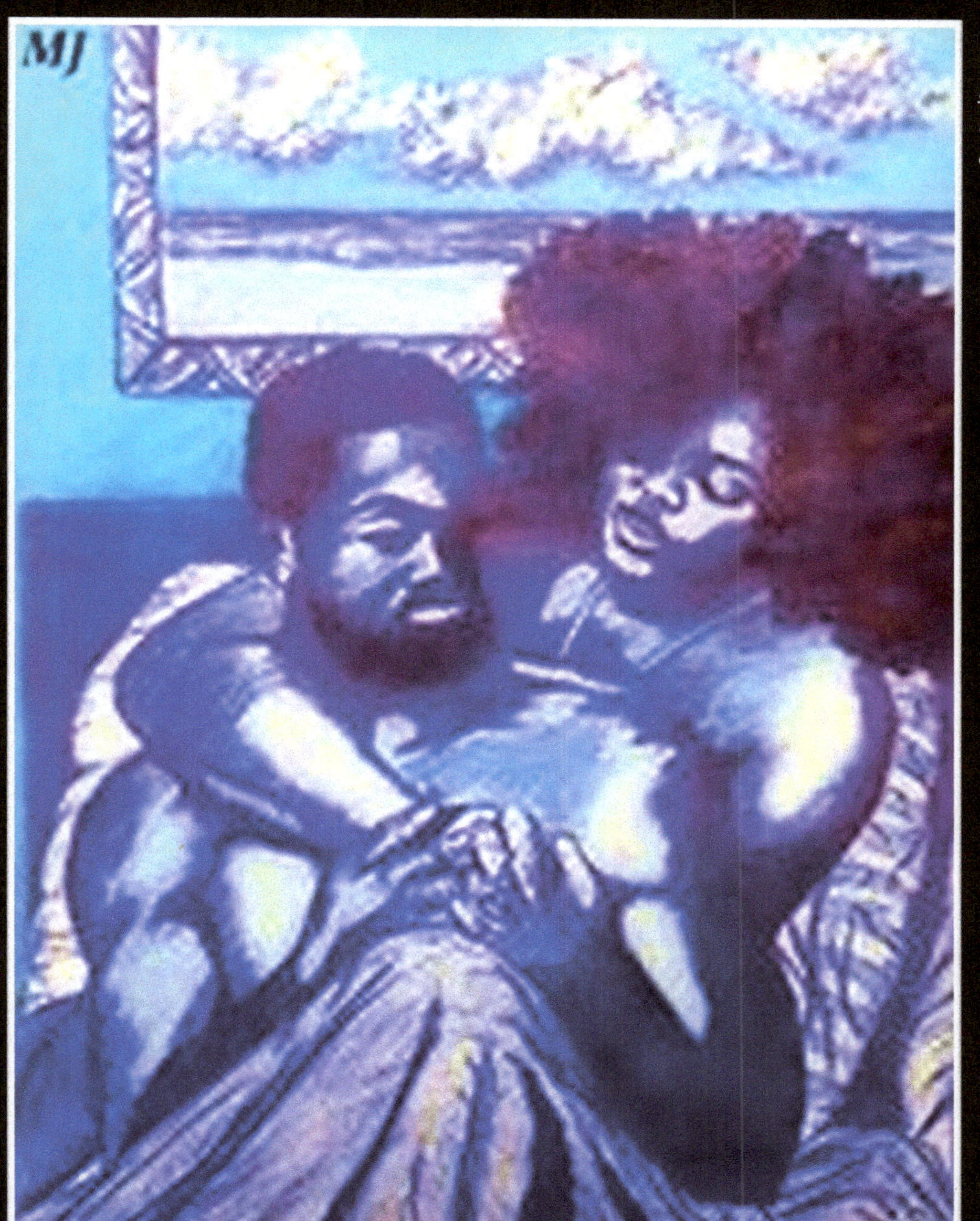

2017
Ballpoint Pen and
Colored Pencil

This black love themed portrait shows a couple in bed enjoying each other's time in intimacy displaying physical touch. She is holding him, letting him know that she has his back. Showing each other support is very important in any relationship which is why I gave the drawing this title.

R.A.W. (Portrait of Big Daddy Kane)

2017
Graphite and Colored Pencil

I am a big fan of Hip-Hop. Growing up, the best show to watch the latest hip-hop was on Video Music Box or Yo MTV Rap. One of the artists that I saw a lot of was Big Daddy Kane. His rhyming style was unique and he, along with Rakim, encouraged other rappers to step their game up.

When I created this portrait of Kane, I thought about his hit song, R.A.W. Here the words to his song is written beside Kane's face and the title of the song in big bold letters to better describe how dope his skills are as an emcee.

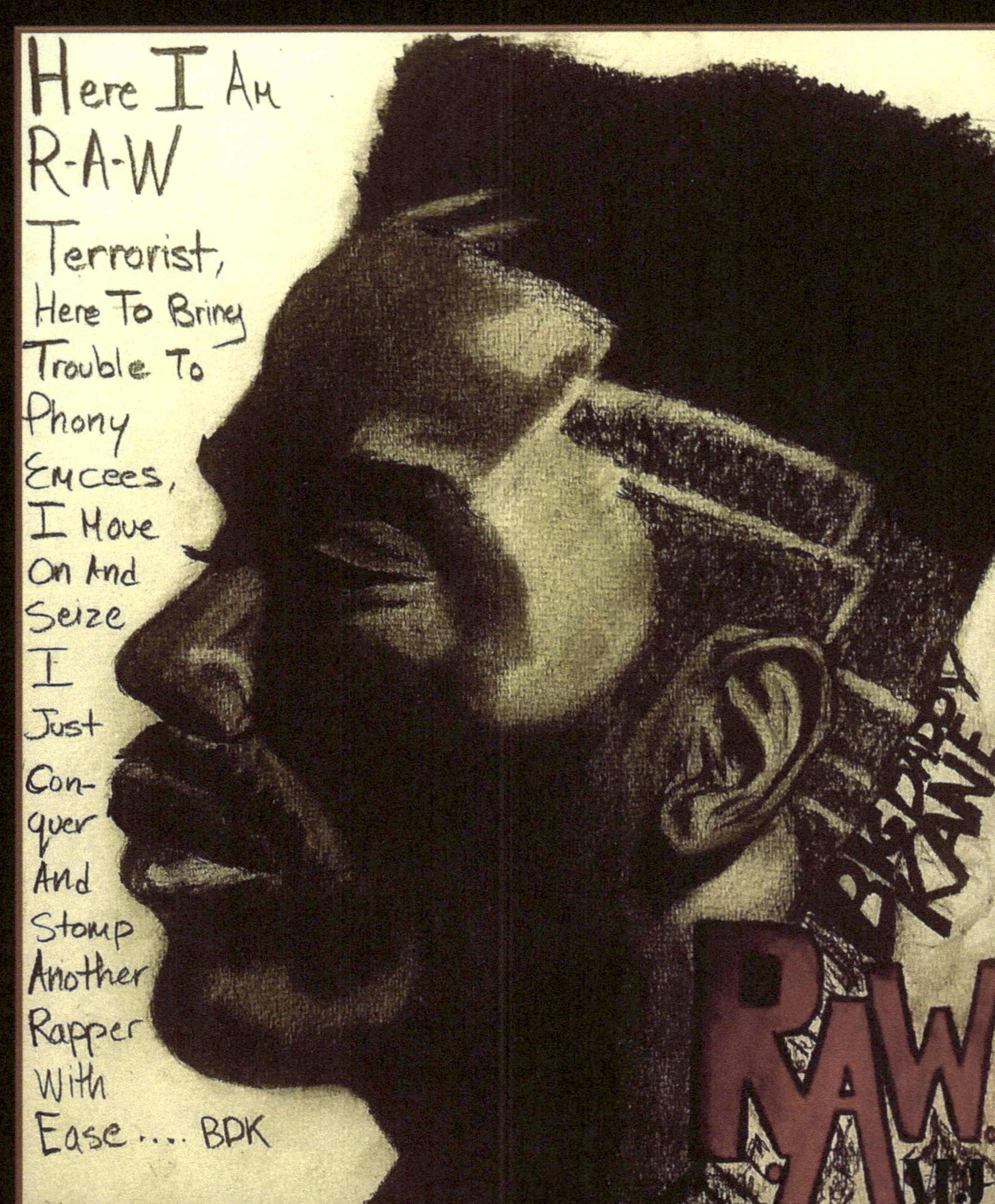

Tree of Pride

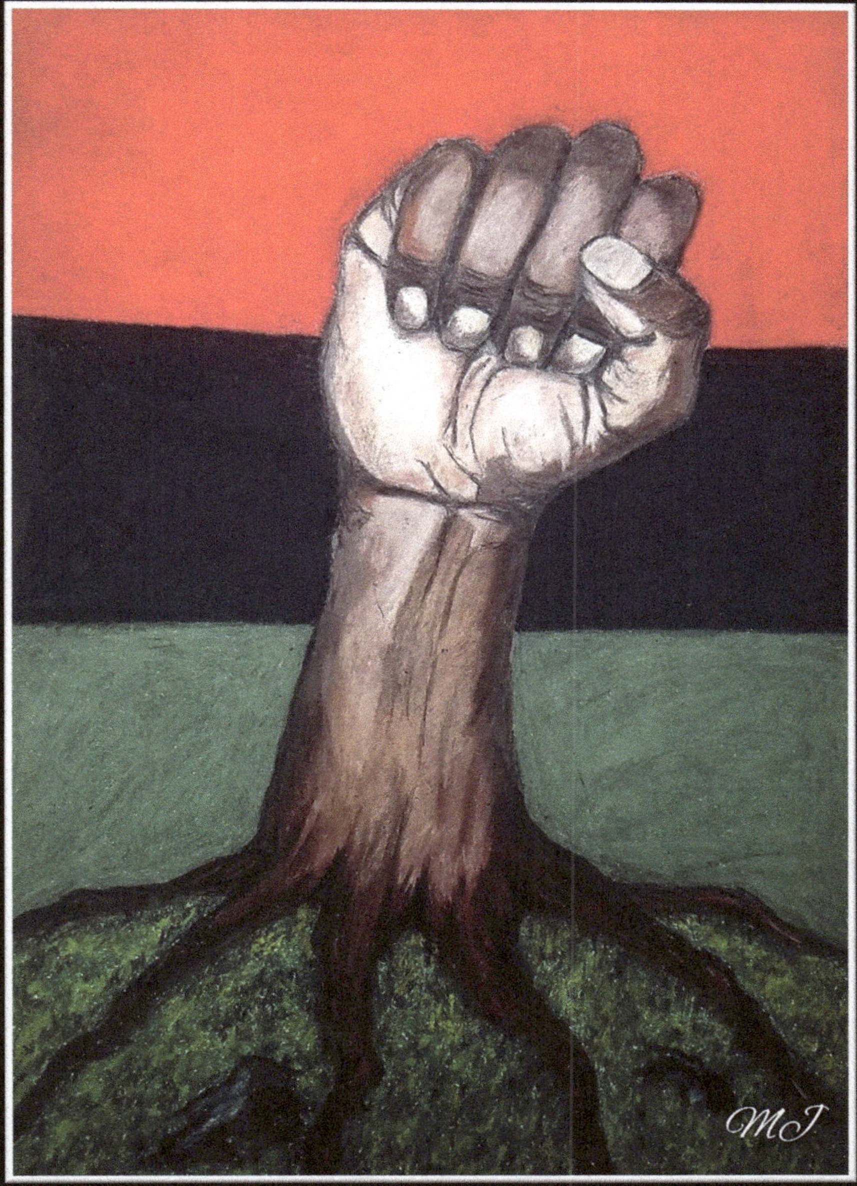

2017
Colored Pencils and Oil Pastels

This drawing is very important to me because it best expresses how deep I love my culture and love being black. During the process of creation, my first idea was to just draw a portrait of rap-artist and activist, Chuck D from Public Enemy, but I couldn't get the proportion of his arm right and feeling myself getting frustrated was about to toss it in the trash. Something inside me told me to stop, I dug deep and suddenly thought about my people and what we have been through for generations, the major accomplishments, contributions and overall, the love for my people. At that point I knew exactly what to drew. The statement I want to make with this piece is that I am proud of who I am,

Natural Mystic (Portrait of Bob Marley)

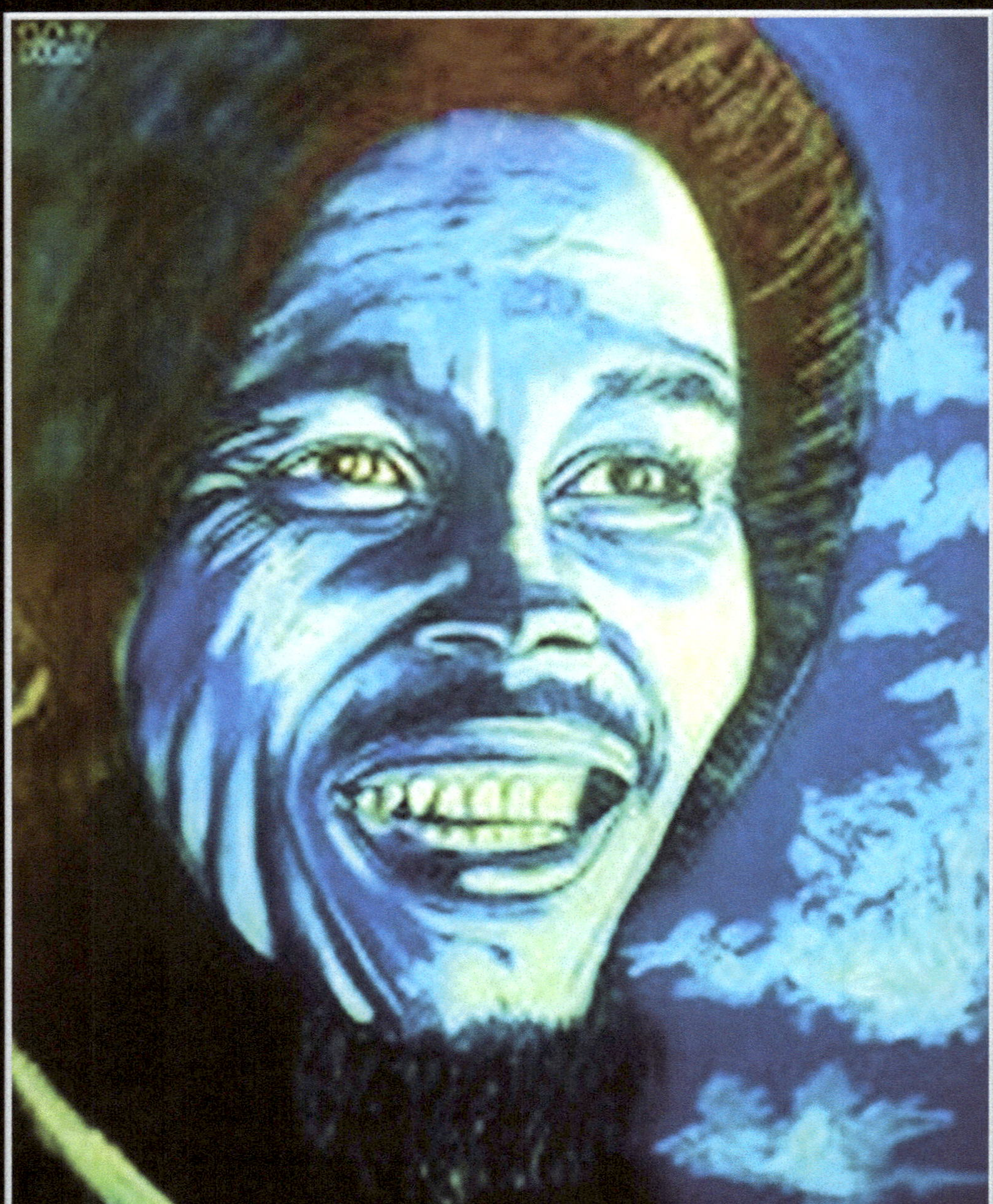

2017
*Colored Pencils
and Oil Pastels on
toned paper*

*I am a huge fan of
Bob Marley and I
have created many
portraits of him but
this one I would have
to say is my most
realistic one.*

*If you look closely, in
the clouds a lion is
seen to symbolize the
Rastafarian religion.*

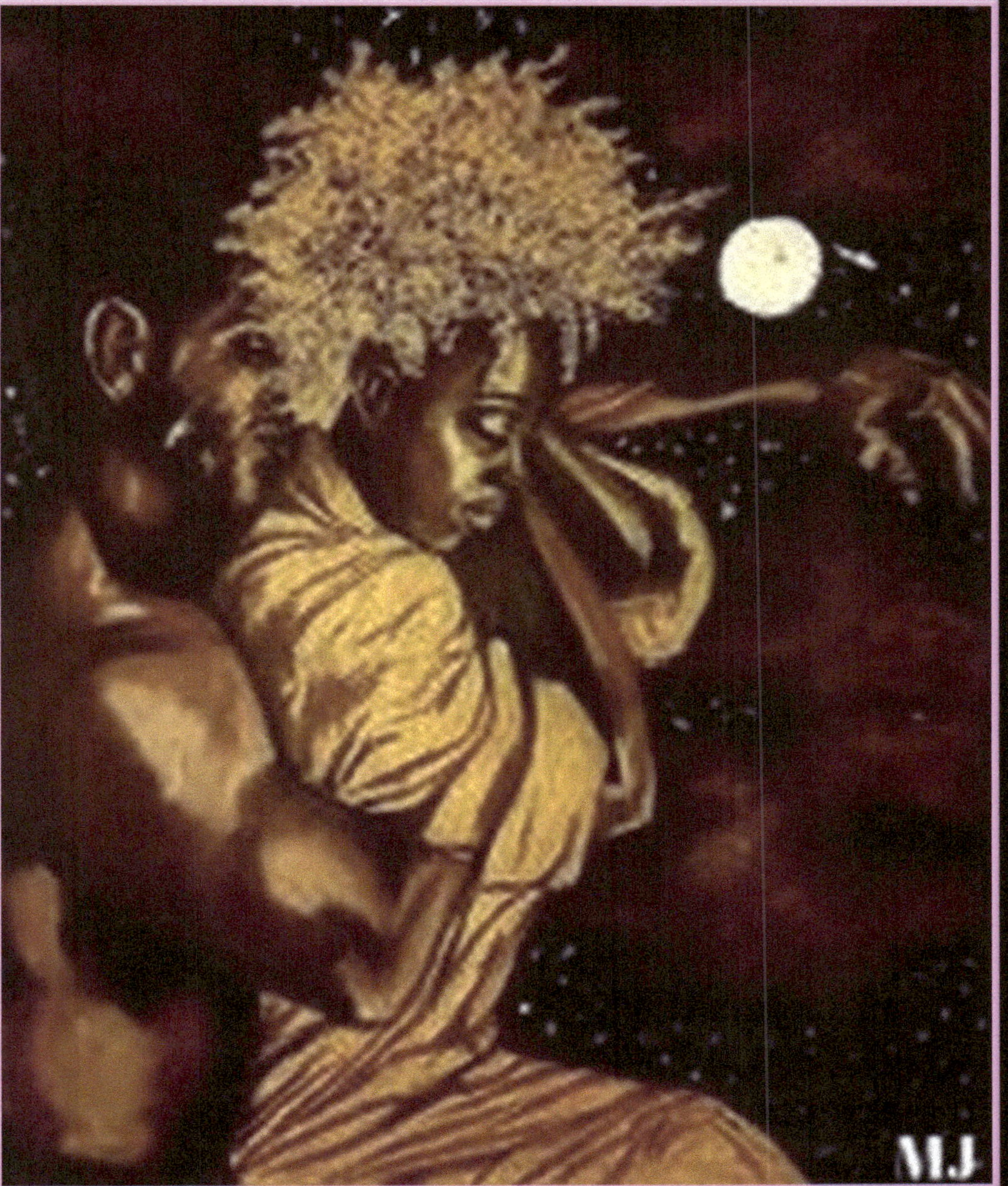

2017
Colored Pencils and
Oil Pastels on paper

This black love themed
portrait shows a couple
embraced while in deep
sleep.

In the background is the
night sky filled with
stars.

MJ

The King Taking Care of His Queen

2017
Colored pencils and
pastels

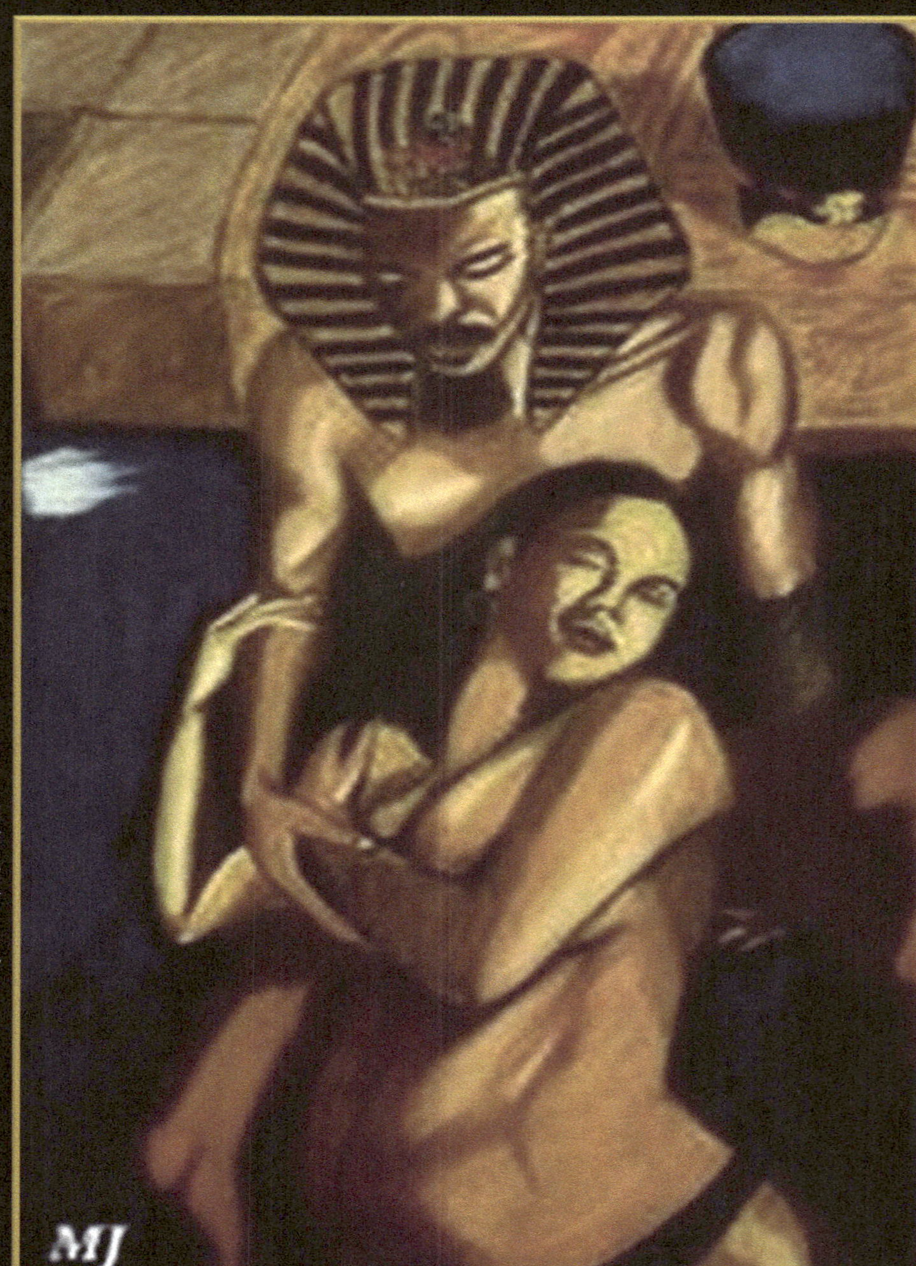

This black love themed portrait was inspired by a photo that I saw of a man in a tub comforting his pregnant partner. I reimagined the man as an Egyptian pharaoh in the water holding his pregnant Queen.

The Redemption of Malcolm X

I admire many black activists; however, Malcolm X has always been my personal favorite. I just love what he stood for and was very inspired by his story and journey. He overcame his painful past, transitioned from a hard criminal to become a person of righteousness. I wanted to show all of this in this portrait.

I have Malcolm centered in the middle. In the clouds shows the three stages of his past. The process took a couple of years to create.

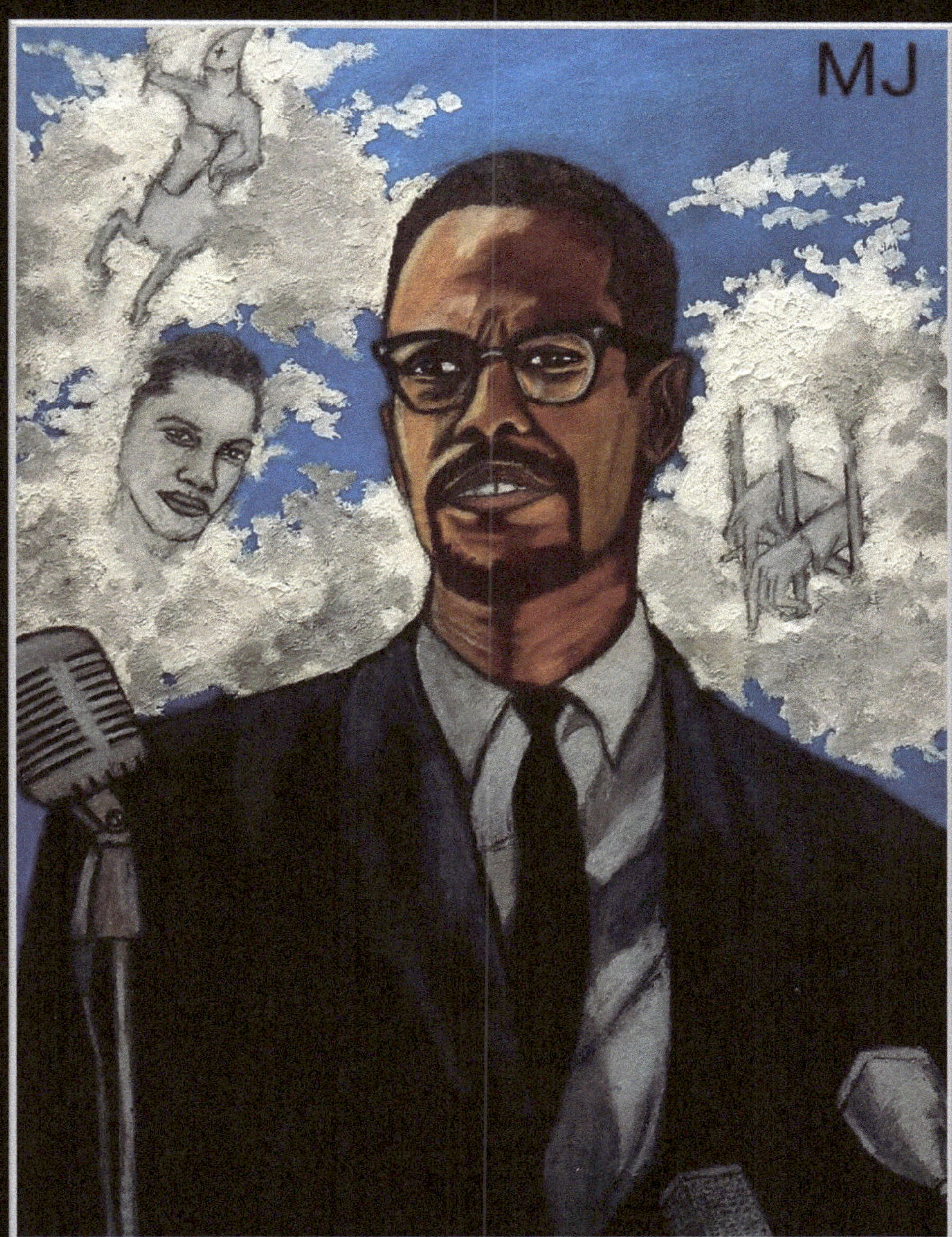

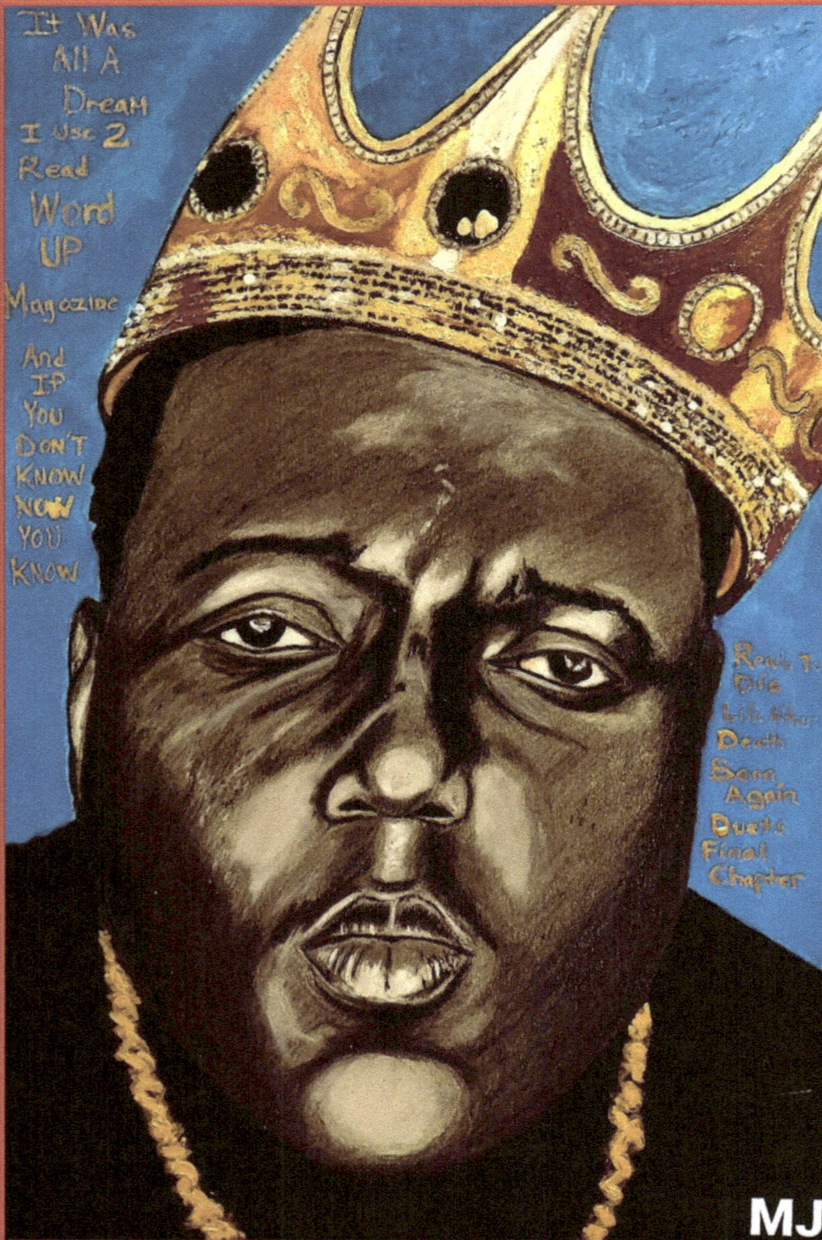

2018
Graphite pencil, colored pencils, oil pastel and acrylic paint

As a big fan of Notorious BIG, I have created many portraits of hm but this one is my best one, plus my personal favorite. When BIG was alive he was called the King of New York, so I drew BIG with his crown which I made gold to make it stand out.

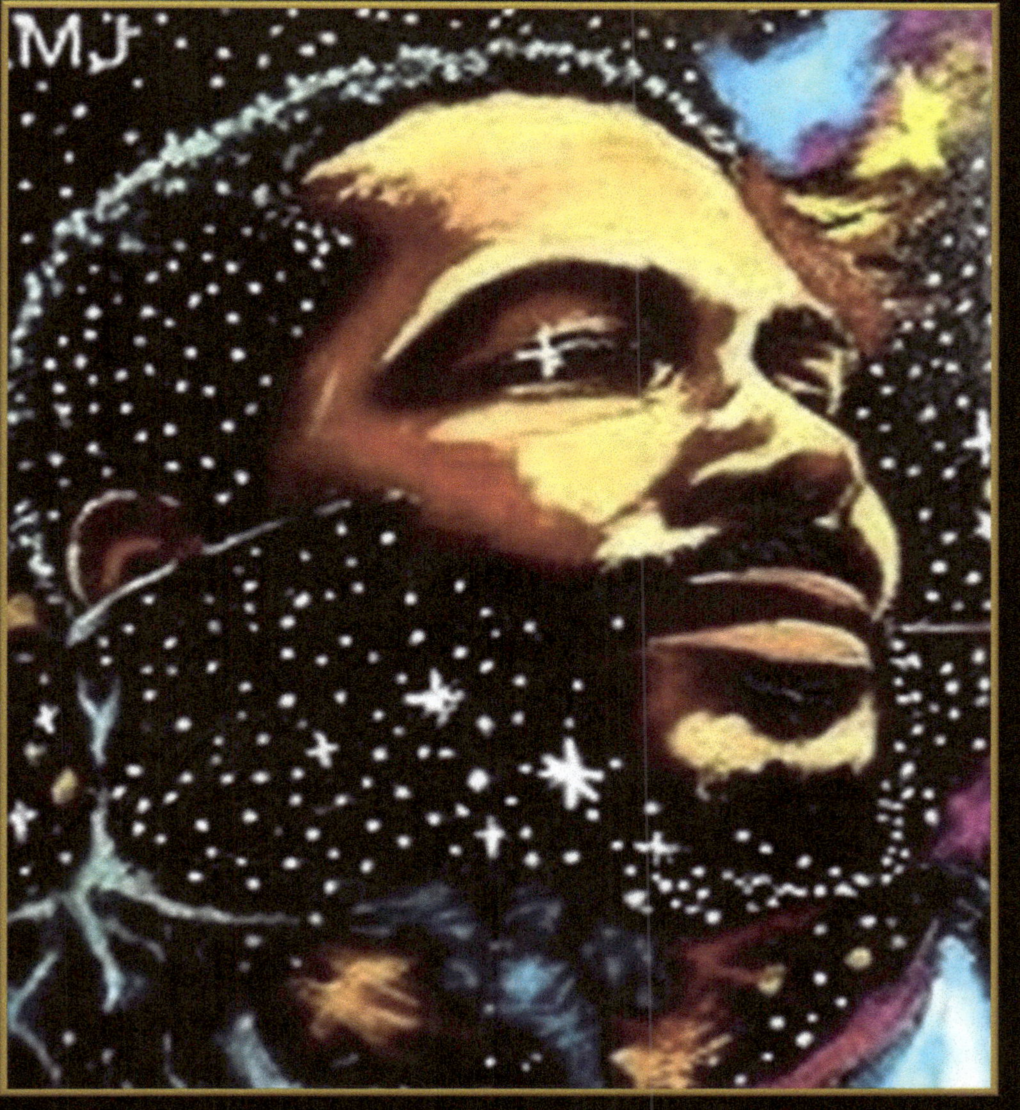

<u>2018</u>
Colored pencils and pastels

In December of 2018 I created this real nice tribute portrait of soul singer, Marvin Gaye, inspired by the cover of his colossal classic album, What's Going On. Around this time, artist Kaden Nelson did a portrait of Marvin Gaye that was chosen as the United States Postal Service stamp, and I was inspired to create this portrait of Marvin imagining if I was the artist chosen to make art for the stamp.

The portrait shows Marvin's face from the album cover in the universe. I wanted to display him as a godly presence.

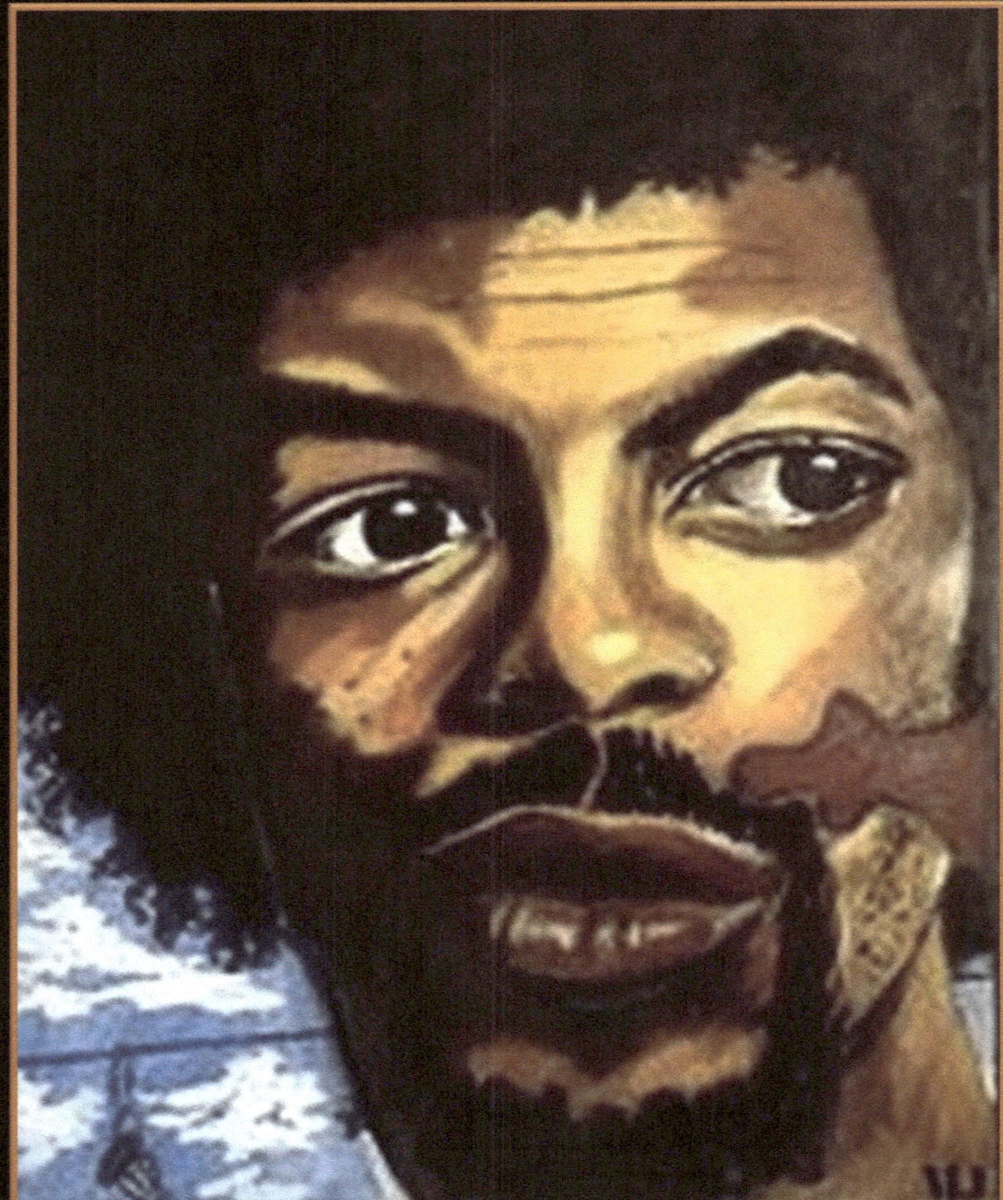

This portrait is of musician and poet, Gil Scott-Heron. His poetry and music were based mostly on racism, life in inner-city, exposing the neglects of America, and more. The portrait is mainly inspired by a song from his second album called, Pieces of a Man. Gil's face is missing a piece as if it's a puzzle.

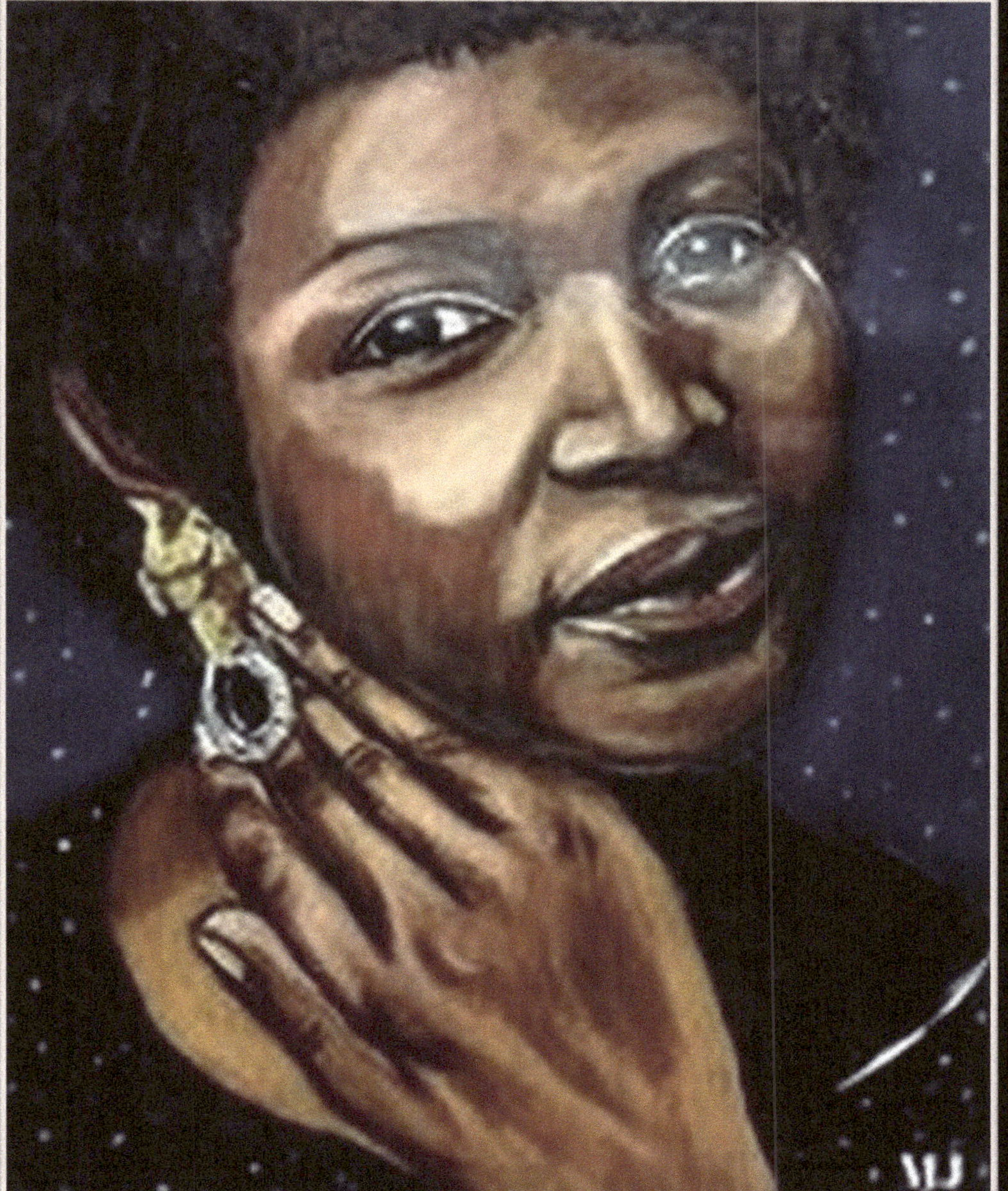

As a fan of one of the greatest singers of all time, I wanted to display Aretha Franklin as a godly presence in the universe.

2018
Colored pencils and
pastels on paper

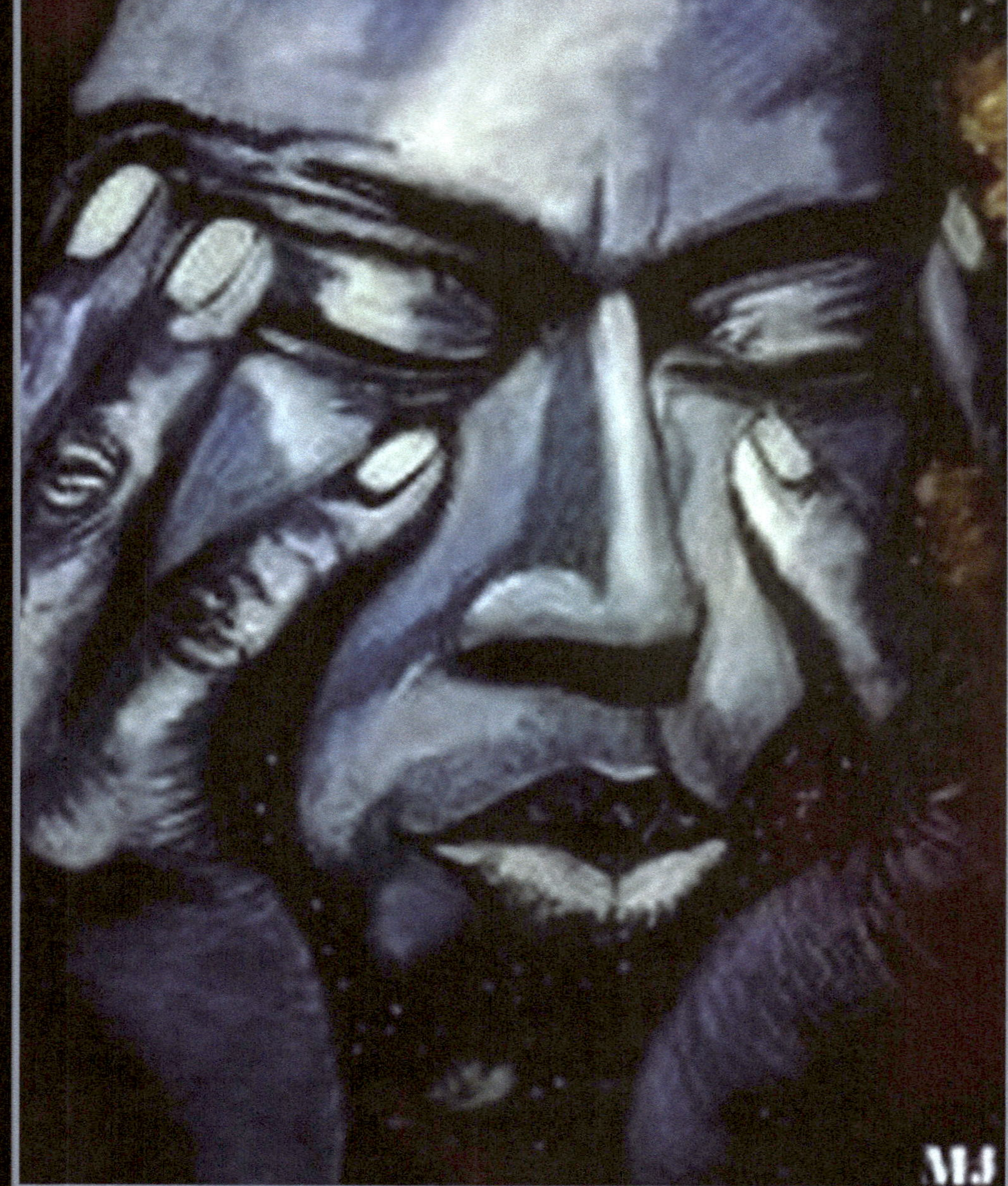

In this portrait, I displayed my favorite jazz trumpet player as a godly presence in the universe. It is inspired by one of the photos that Miles took for his album cover of Tutu.

John Coltrane (Forever Eternal)

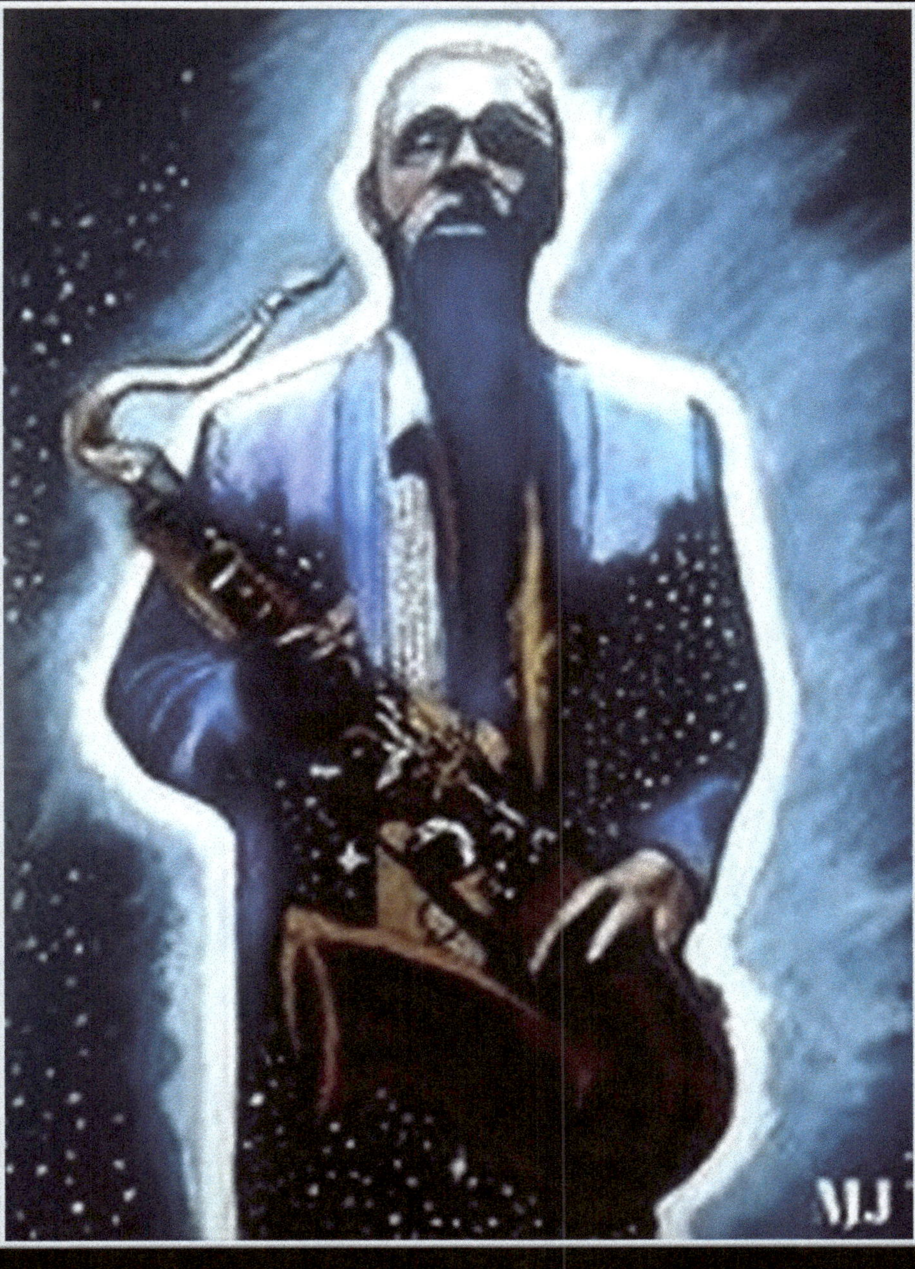

2018

Colored pencils and Oil pastels

I wanted to display my favorite jazz saxophone player, John Coltrane, as a godly presence in the universe.

2018
Pen, Colored pencil,
Oil pastels, and
acrylic paint on paper

In this portrait of John Coltrane, I wrote his most well-known songs and albums that he made with his group, John Coltrane quartet.

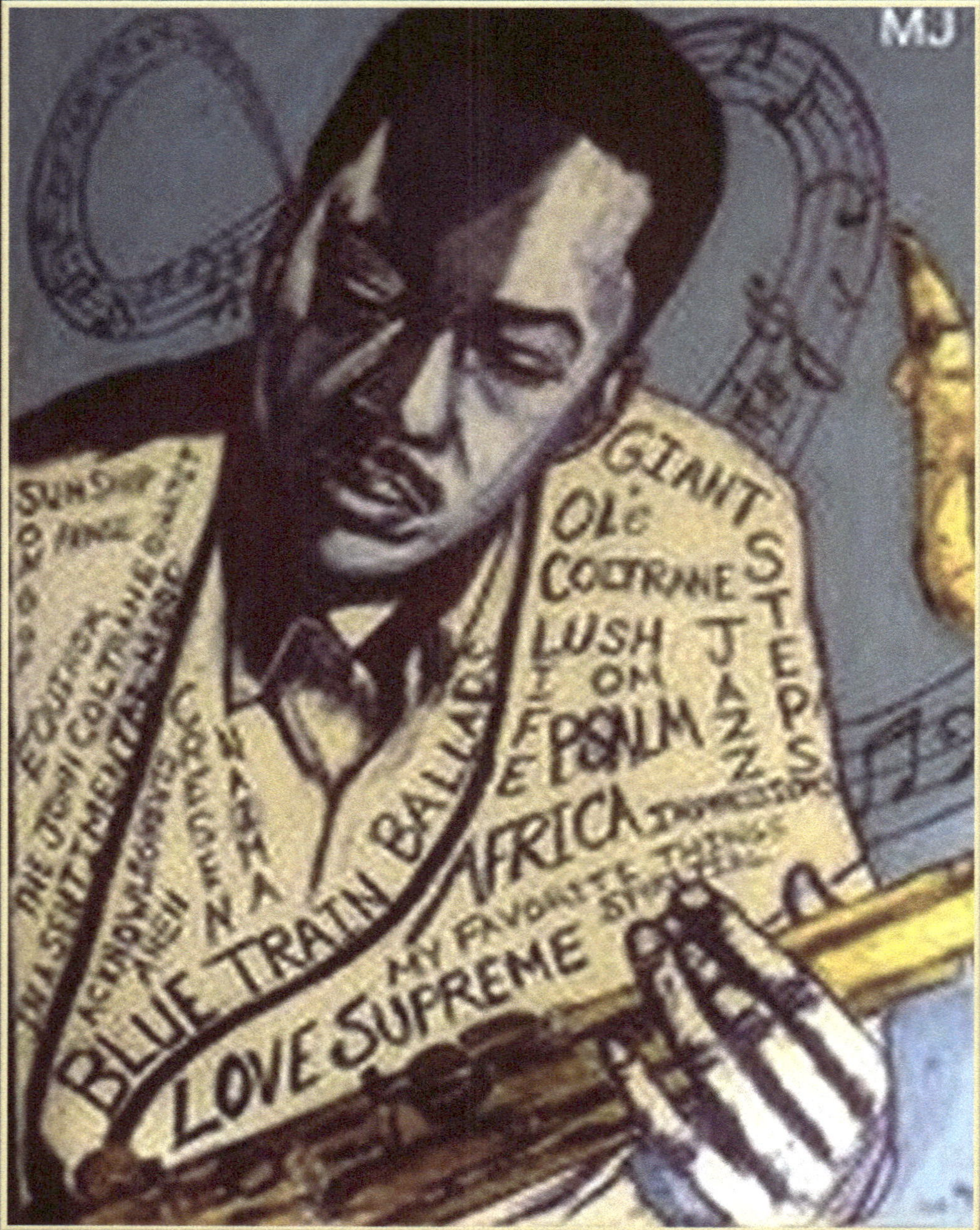

MJ
GIANT
OLÉ
COLTRANE
STEPS
LUSH JAZZ
I OM
E PSALM
SUN SHIP
AFRICA
BALLADS
BLUE TRAIN
MY FAVORITE THINGS
LOVE SUPREME

The World shall Feel My Rage
(Portrait of Erik Killmonger from Black Panther)

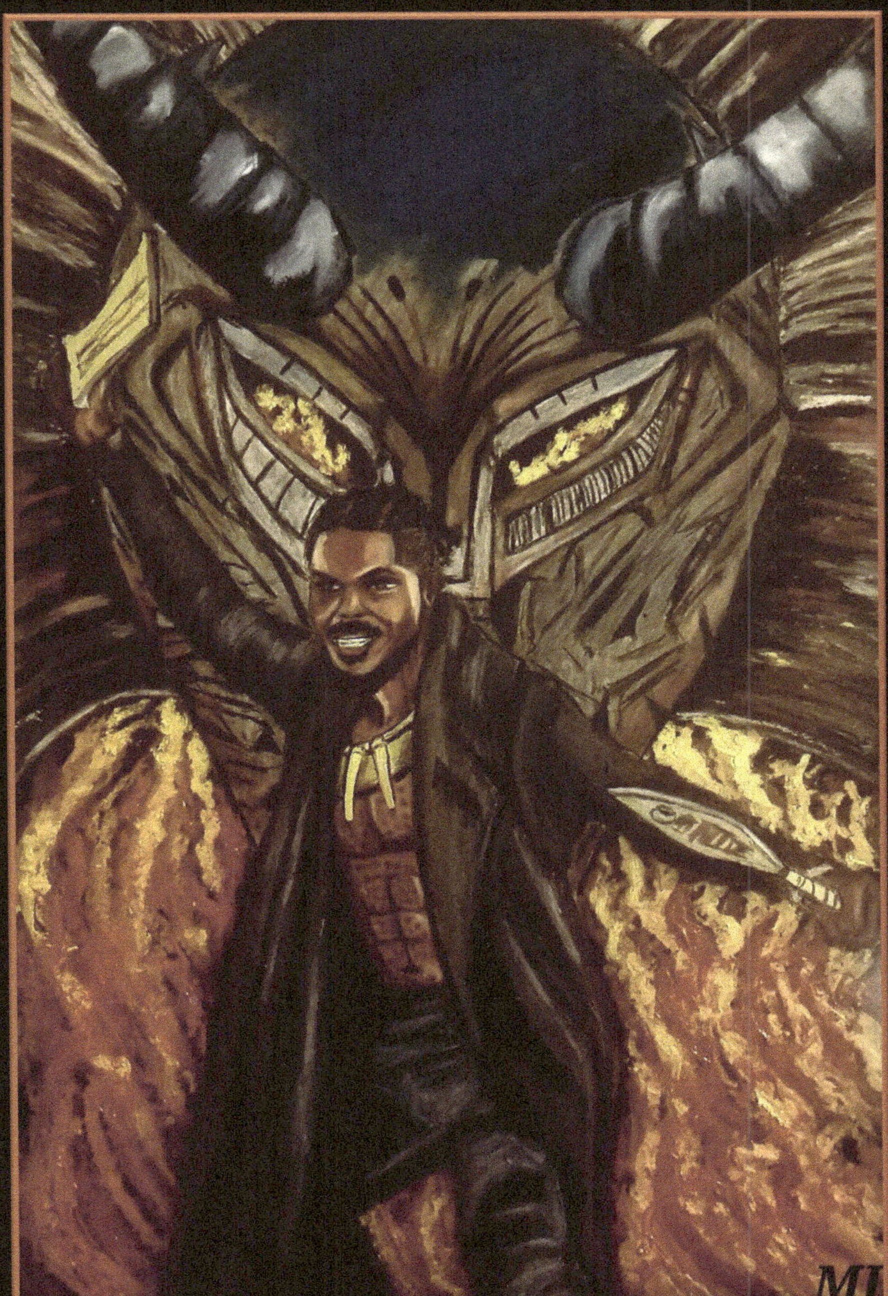

2018
Colored pencils, oil pastels
and acrylic paint on paper

Inspired by the Black Panther film, I drew this portrait of Michael B. Jordan as character, Erick Killmonger. In the movie, Erik is full of rage and wants revenge for the death of his father.

I displayed him in fighting stance holding weapons. Behind him is the African mask that he took from the museum and fire to symbolize the rage that he felt inside.

Portrait of Chadwick Boseman as King TChalla/Black Panther

2018
Colored pencils and oil pastels on wood

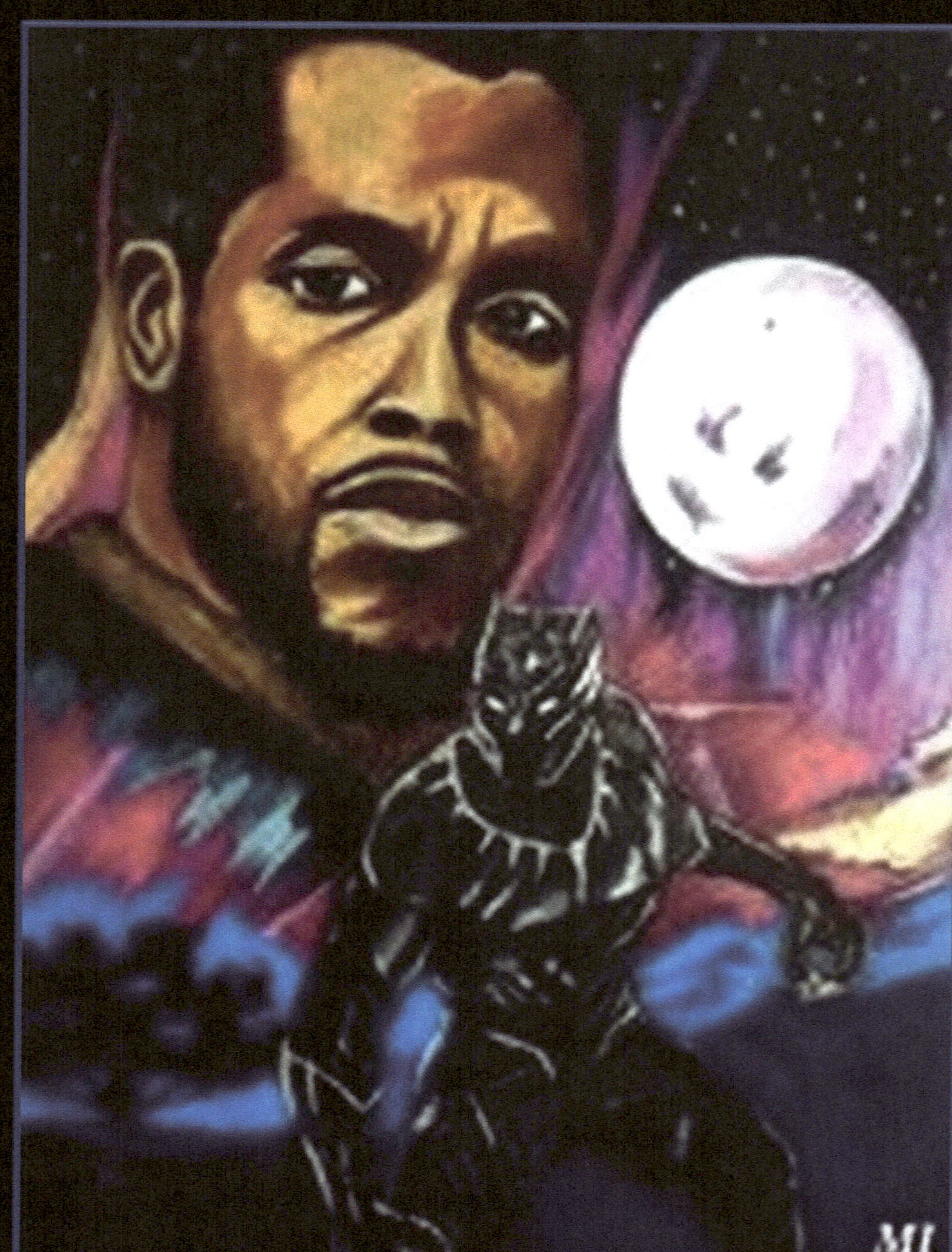

Inspired by the Black Panther film, I drew and painted this portrait of King TChalla/The Black Panther in the ancestral planes.

Portrait of Winston Duke as Mbaku from Black Panther

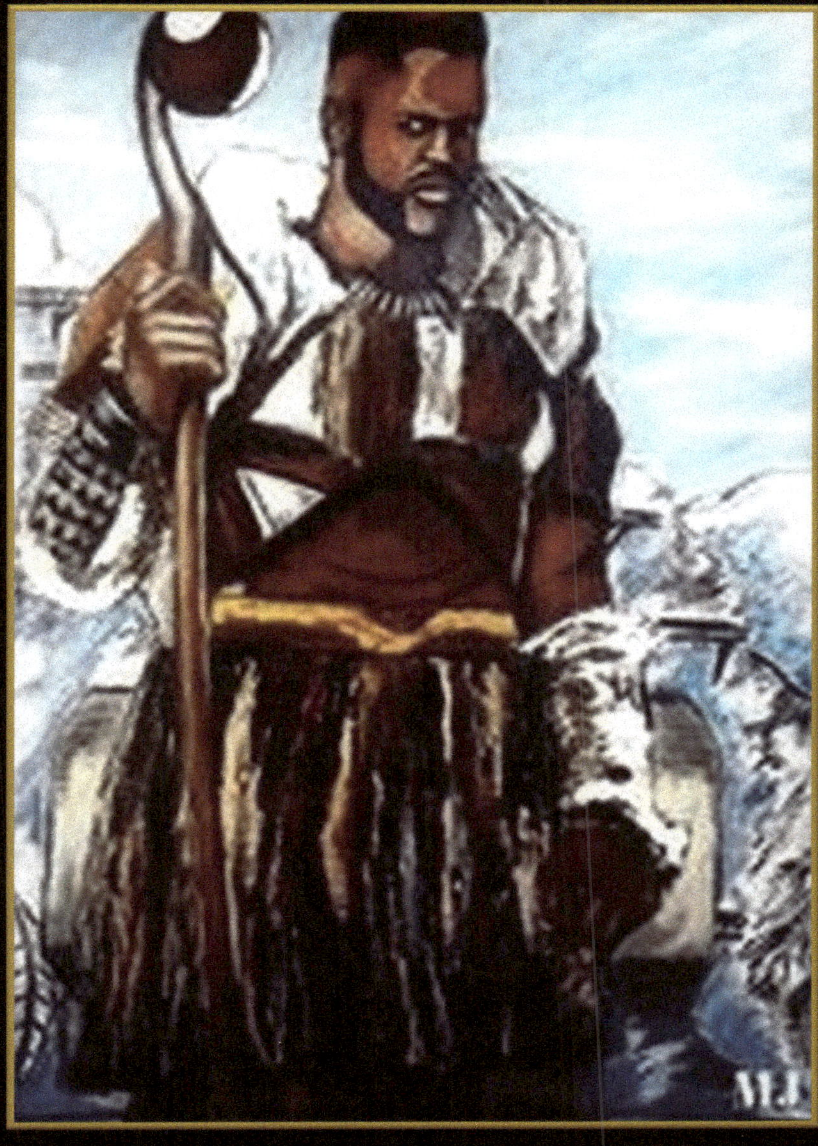

<u>2018</u>
Colored pencils, oil pastels and acrylic paint on paper. 18x24

Inspired by the Black Panther film, this portrait shows character, Mbaku, lord of the Mountain tribe, Jabari who protests TChalla being the new king.

Black Panther film Portrait

2018
Colored pencils, oil pastels, and gold paint marker on paper

18x24

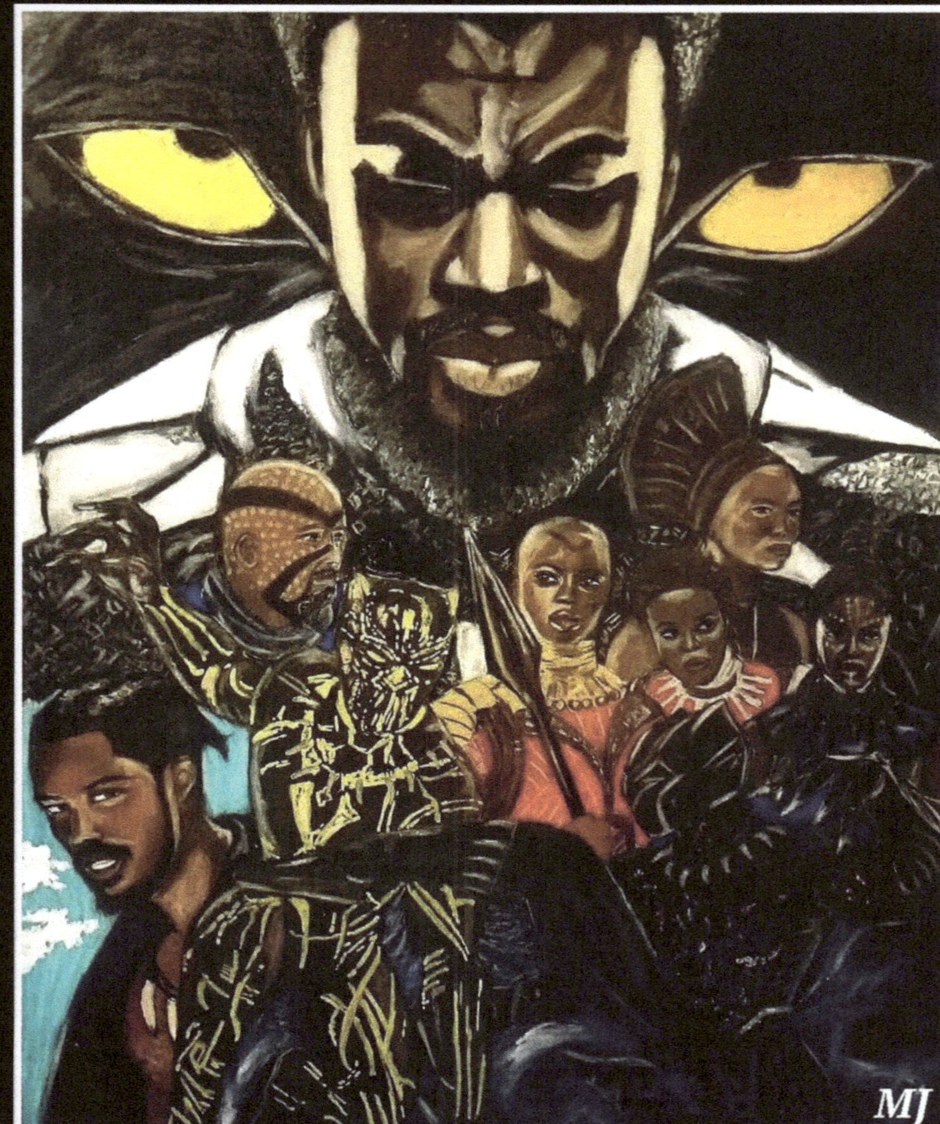

In 2018, one of the best superhero films were made titled, *Black Panther.* This film had a mainly black cast and for the first time, we are displayed in a positive light. I was so proud of the film and was inspired to create a portrait dedicated to the main cast.

Tree of Love

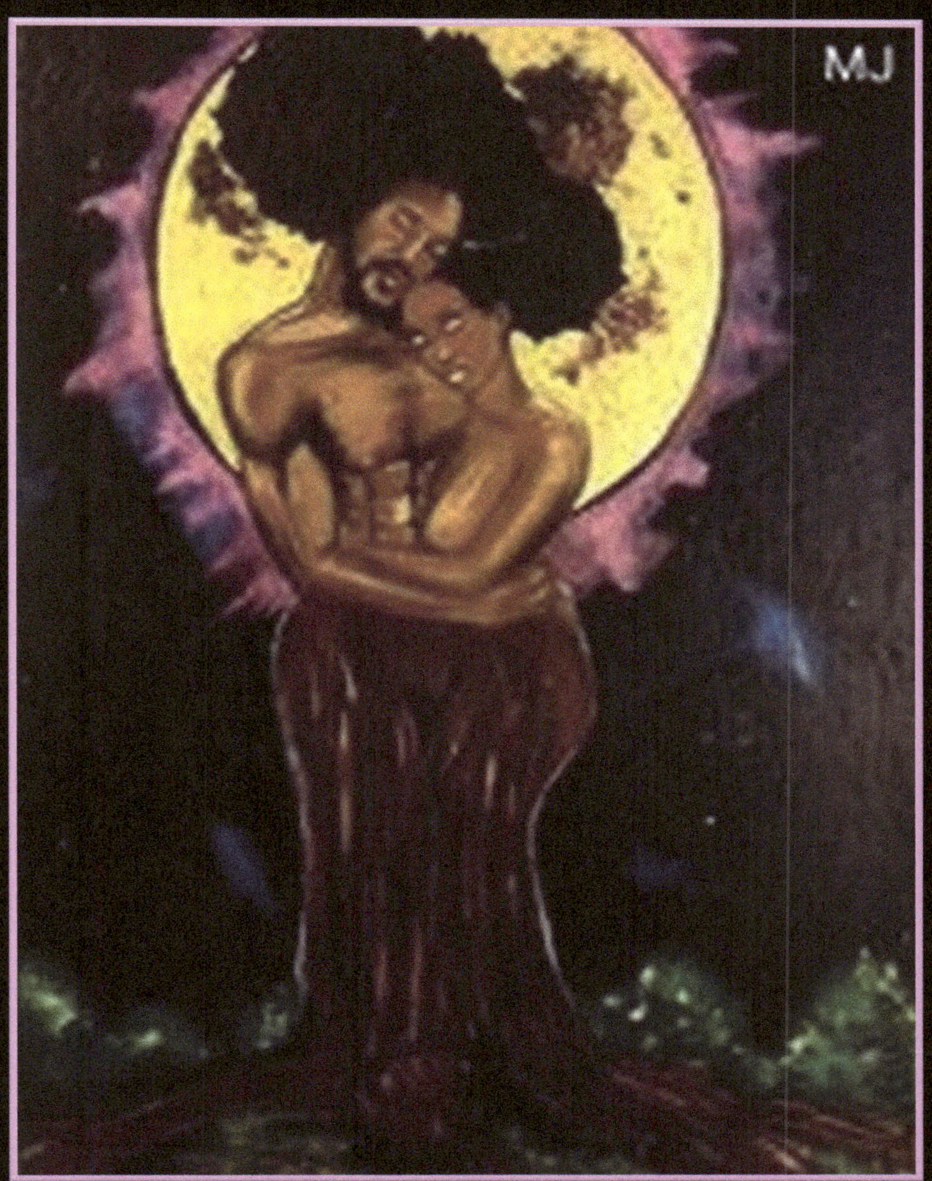

2018
Colored pencils, oil pastels, oil and acrylic paint on wooden canvas board. 12x16

This black themed portrait shows a couple hugged together in an embrace while at the same time they are in the form of a tree, which is why I named it, The Tree of Love.

I look at love and companionship as how trees grow firm and strong. Two people in love growing together as one team strong in love, trust, and reaching goals together to build a legacy.

2018

Colored pencils, oil pastels
and acrylic paint on wood
canvas.

12x16

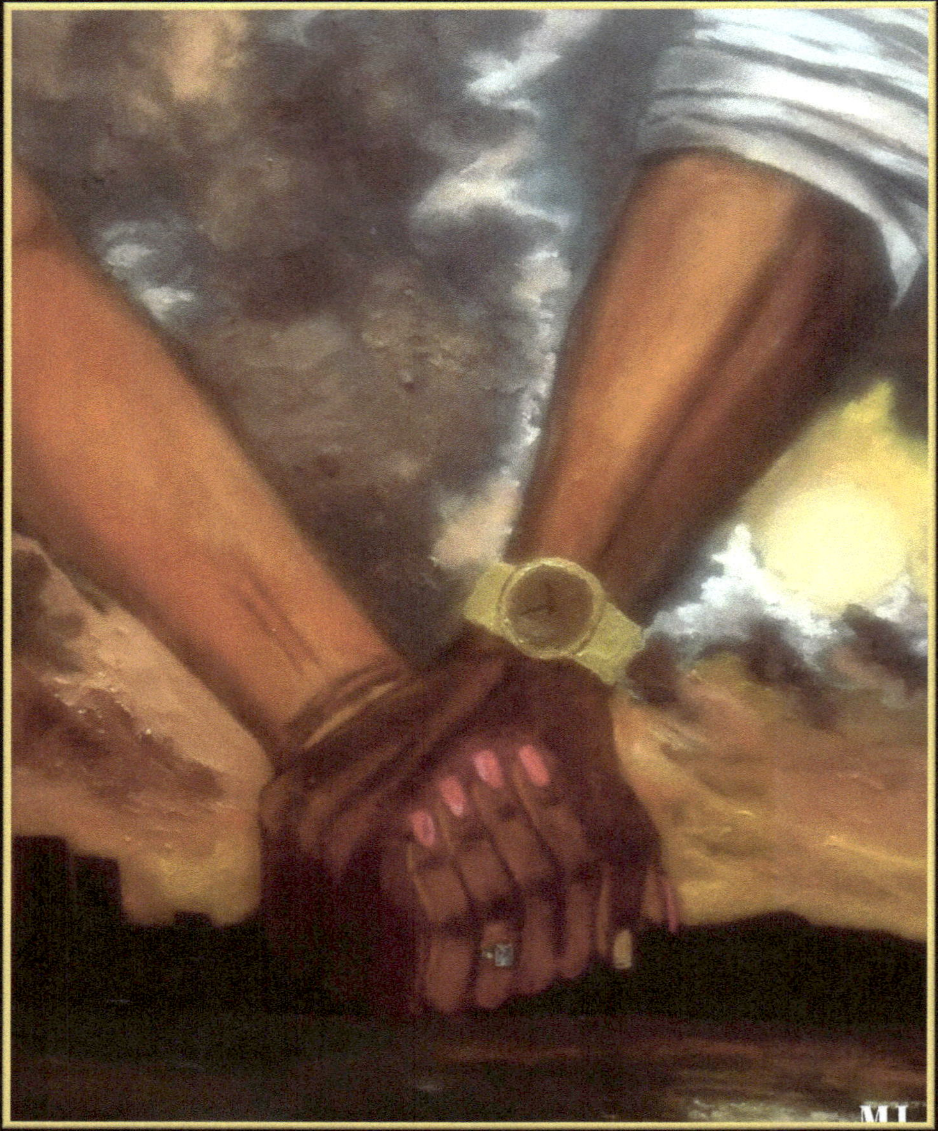

This is a black loved themed
painting, inspired by a poem
that I wrote. It shows a man's
hand holding a woman's hand
and they both take a leap of faith
in love.

We Can't Win

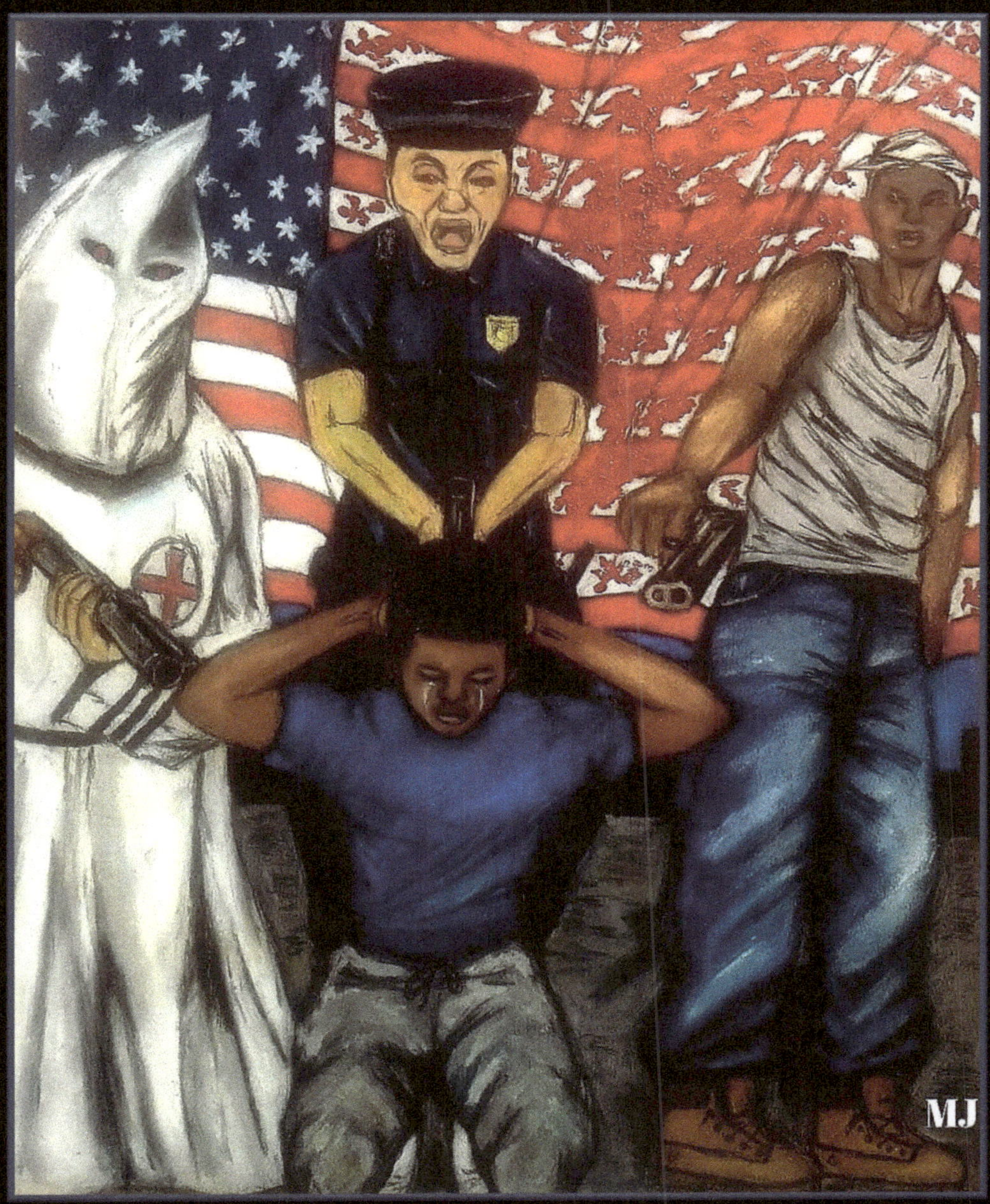

2018
Colored pencils, oil pastels and acrylic paint. 12x16

I have always been passionate about racism and violence committed against my people. With this painting I wanted to share my feelings on this sensitive topic. I titled it, We Can't Win, because it feels like we are not safe anywhere.

In the painting a young black boy is on his knees with his hands behind his head. Behind him are three men with guns pointed at his head. A KKK man, a cop, and a black man. Each man has red eyes to symbolize the rage and hatred they have inside. The American flag in the background has red specs to represent the extreme bloodshed and the violent history of black people in America.

Rasta Man Live Up (Portrait of Bob Marley)

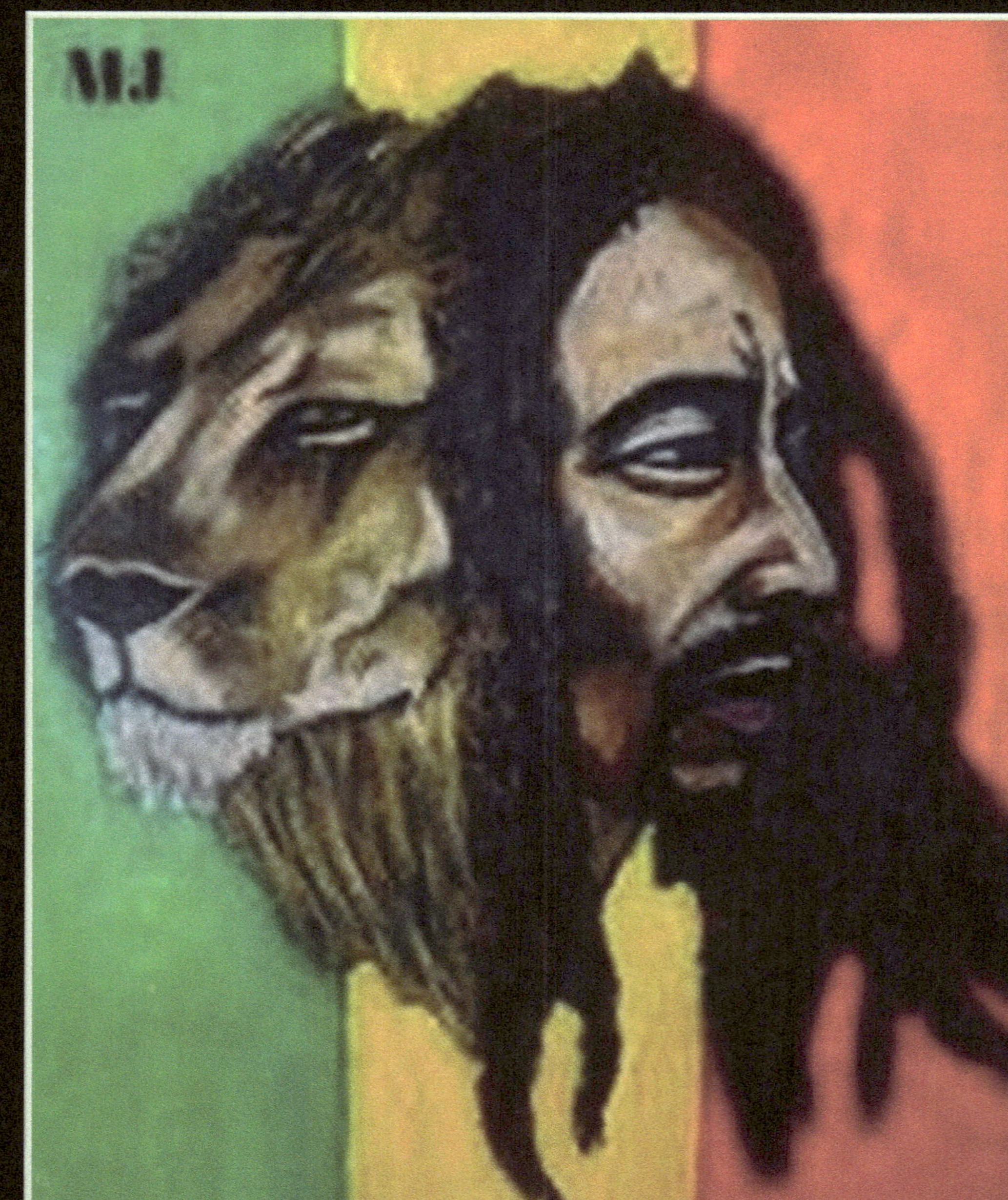

2018
Colored pencils,
oil pastels and oil
paint. 9x12

With this portrait of singer Bob Marley, I wanted to focus on the Rastafarian religion that he practiced for most of his life and career. I attached his head along with the head of a lion which is the symbol of the religion along with the colors in the background.

A Portrait of A Tribe Called Quest

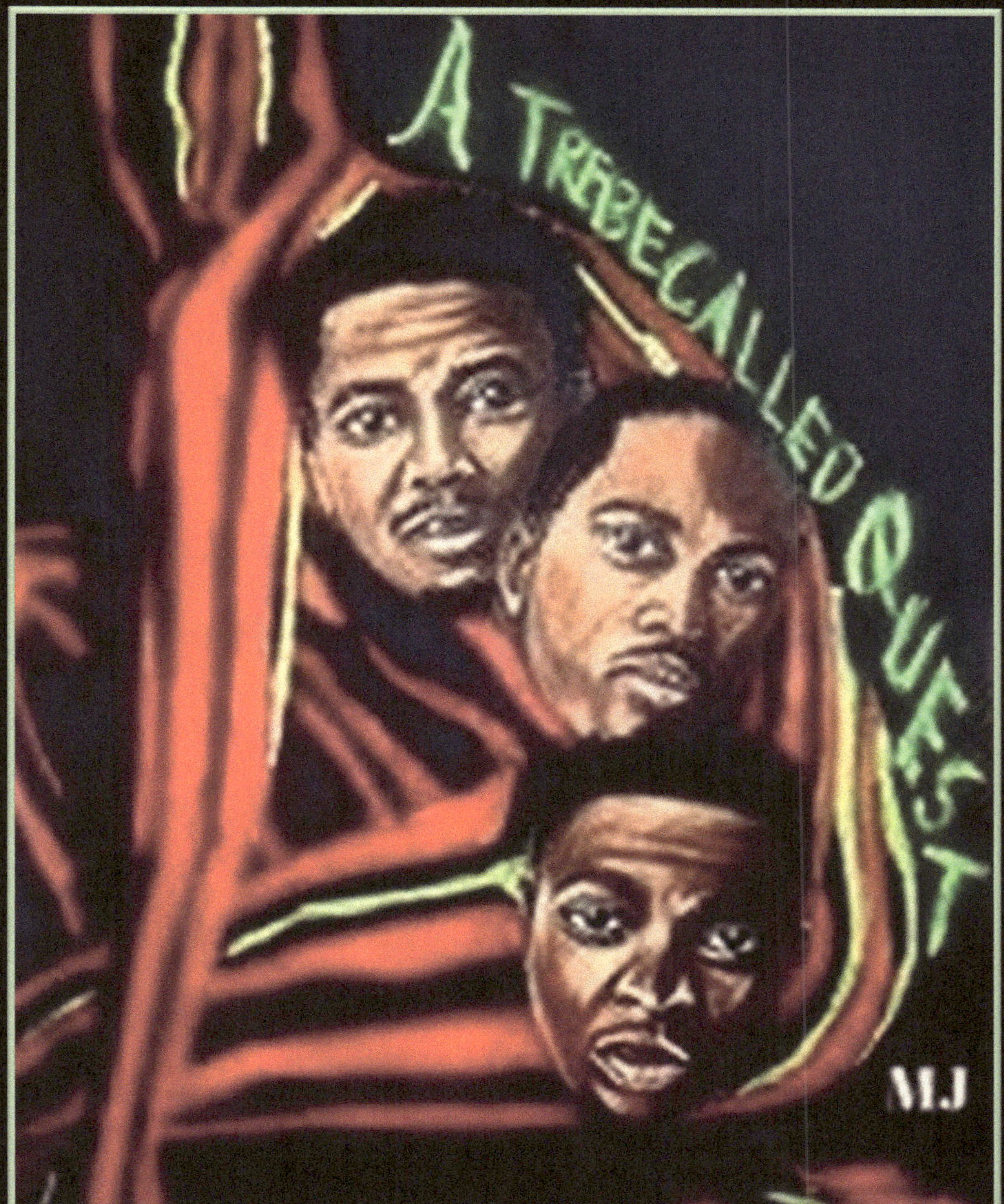

<u>2018</u>
Colored pencils and oil pastels on paper.

9x12

This portrait is a dedication to one of my favorite Hip-Hop groups, ATCQ (A Tribe Called Quest). When I drew the portrait, it was the 25th anniversary of their album, Midnight Marauders. Rest in peace to Phife Dawg.

You Are Royalty

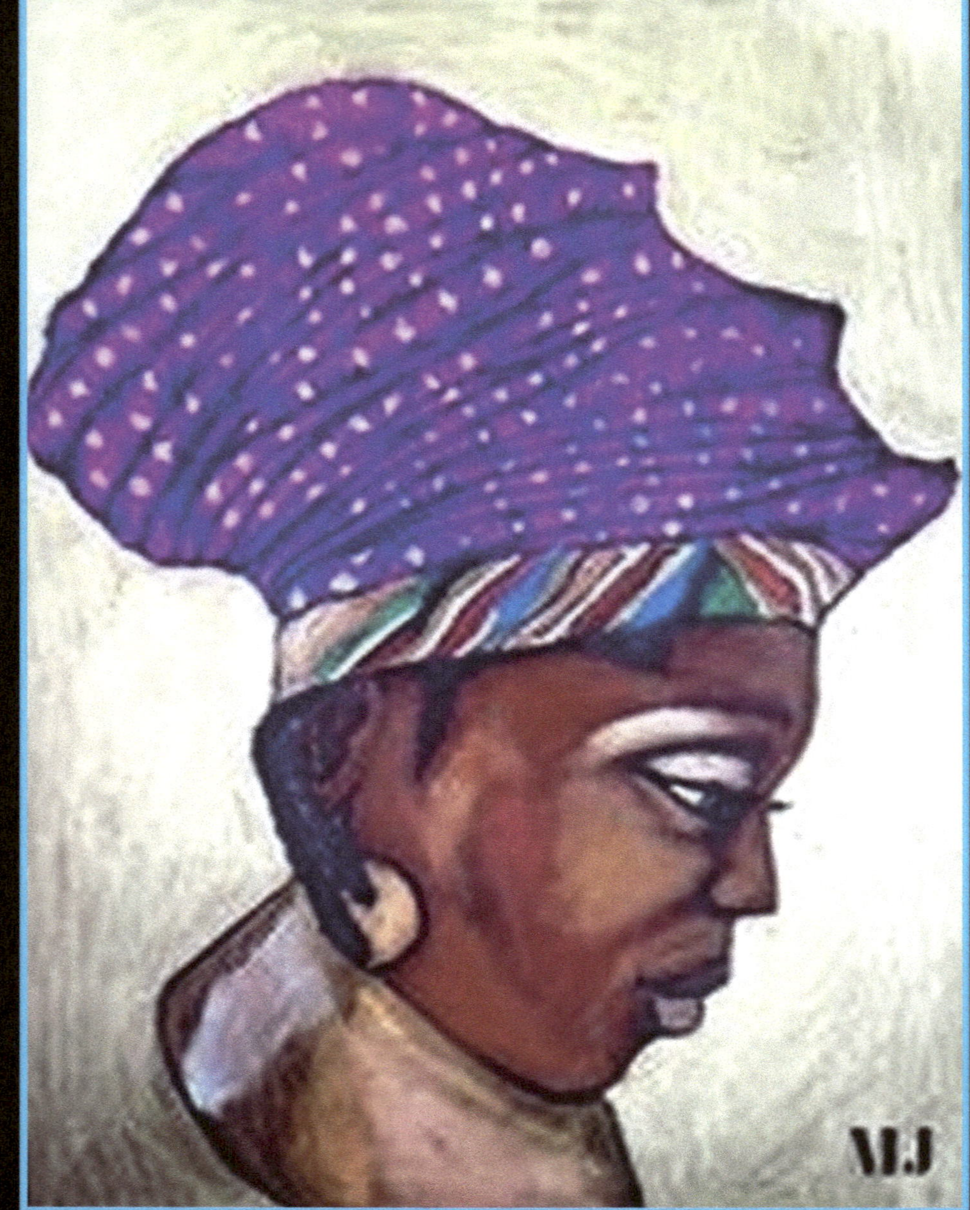

This portrait shows a black woman with a head wrap. She is in the shape of the continent of Africa.

I displayed her as a Queen to express my belief that we as black people should think highly of ourselves.

Portrait of Prodigy

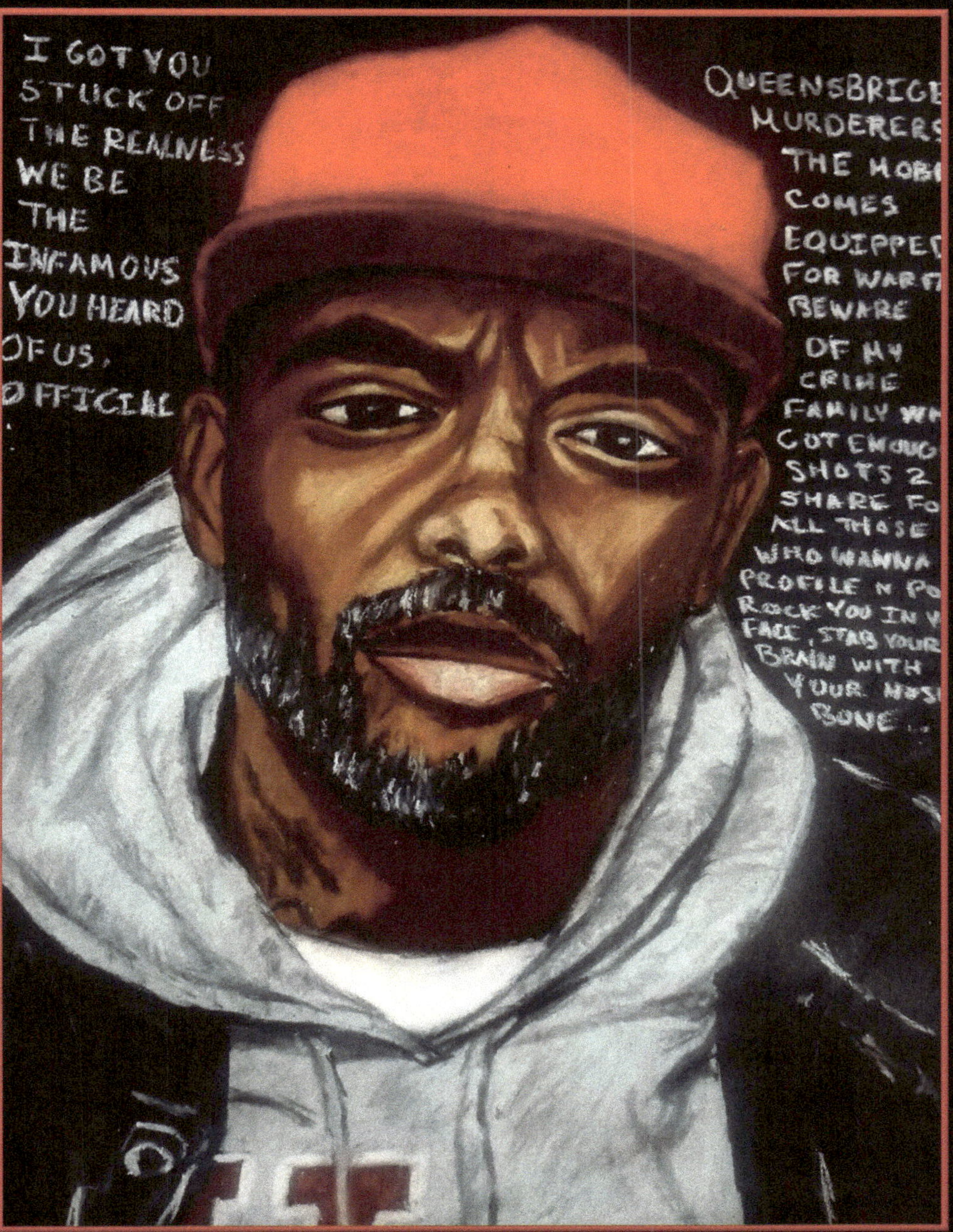

2018
Colored pencils, oil pastels and oil paint on paper. 9x12

This portrait is a dedication tribute to the memory of Hip-Hop artist and member of Mobb Deep, Prodigy. Beside him are the lyrics from Mobb Deep groups most famous song, Shook Ones.

2018
Colored pencils,
oil pastels on
canvas.
9x12

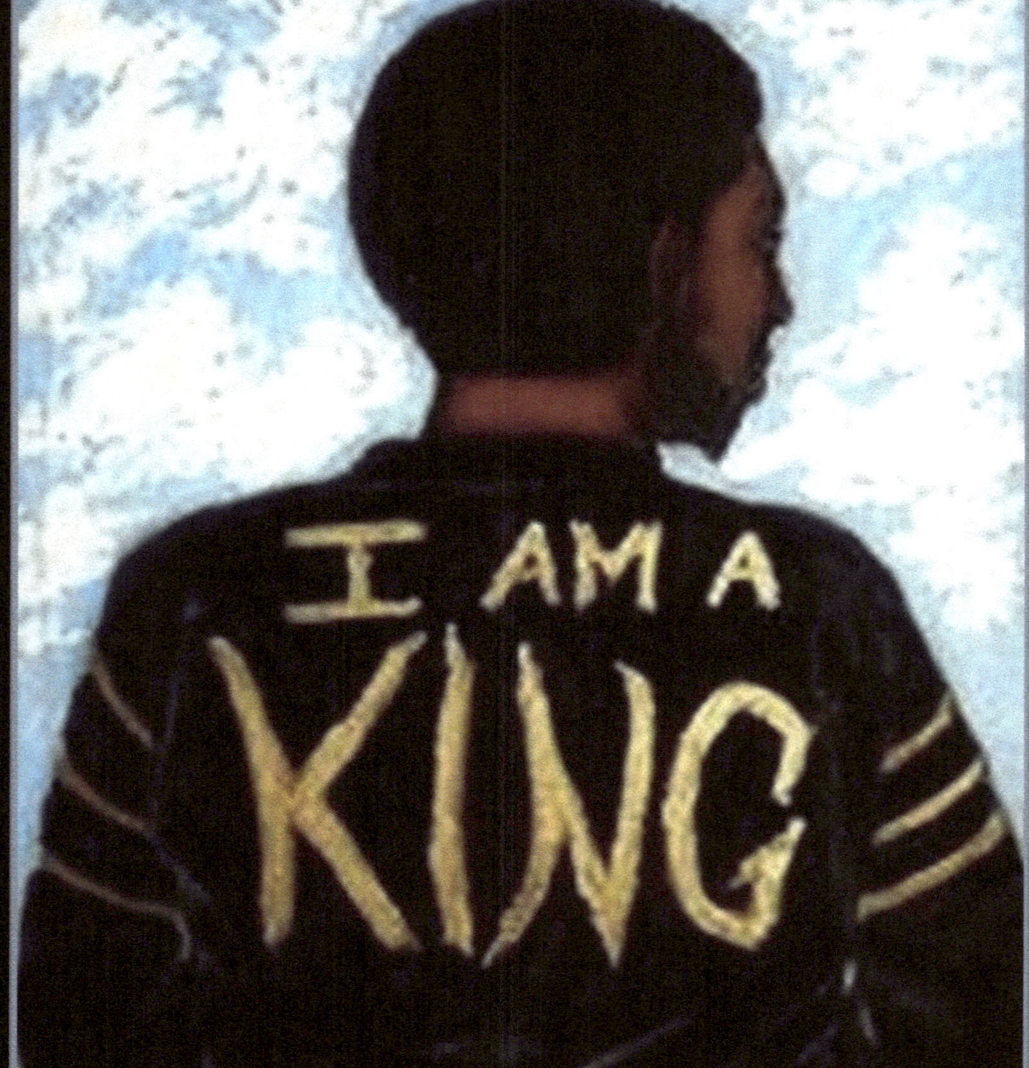

I AM A
KING

Together We Can Stand the Rain

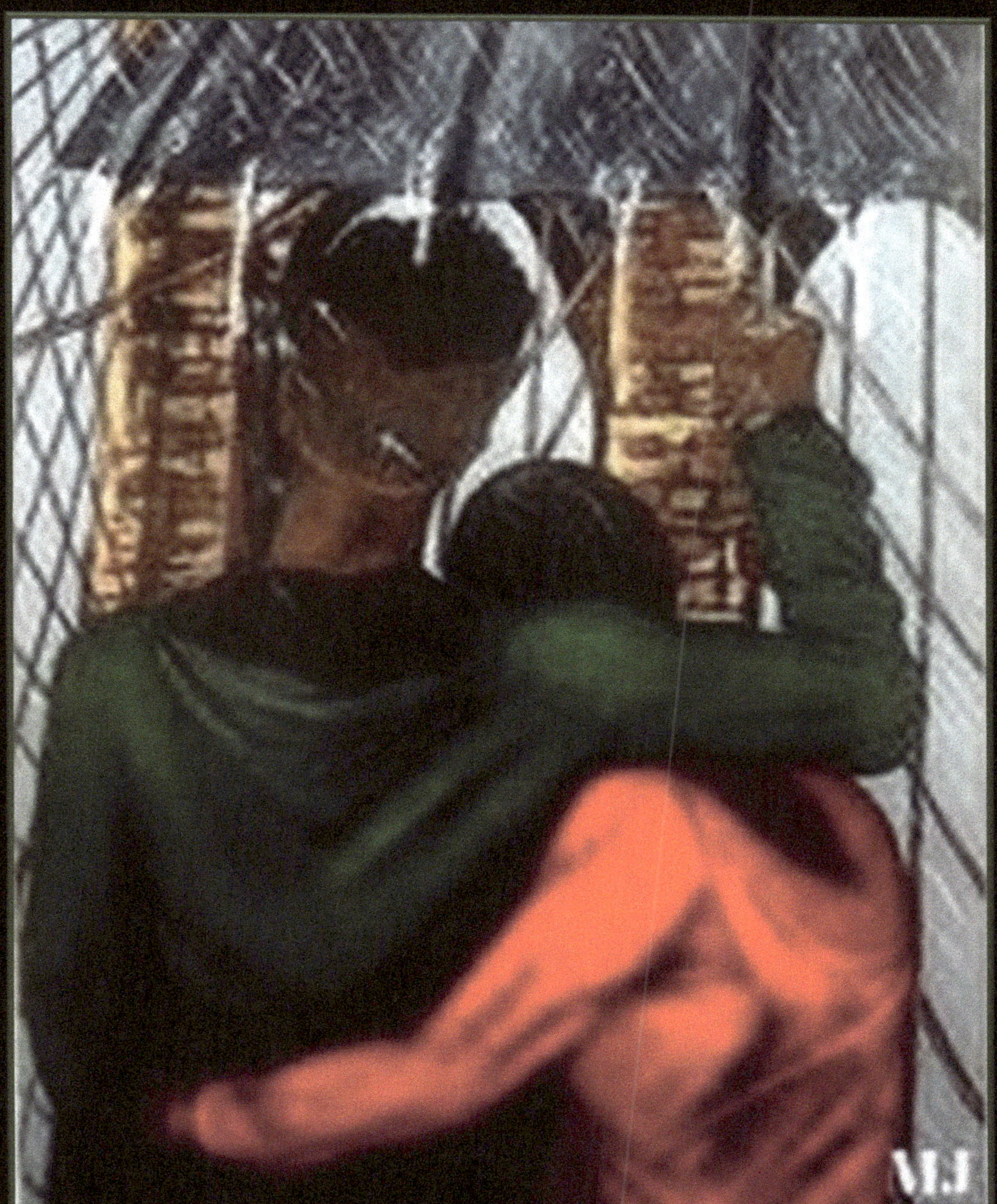

2018
*Colored pencils, oil
pastels on paper.*

*We all know that love
and relationships are
beautiful, but they can
get tough at times. The
tough part is really
what tests the love
between two people in
a relationship.*

*In this black love
themed painting, I
wanted to touch on
this subject by
drawing and painting
a couple hugged
together as they walk
under an umbrella on
the Brooklyn Bridge.
The rain symbolizes
the tough times.*

Black Icons

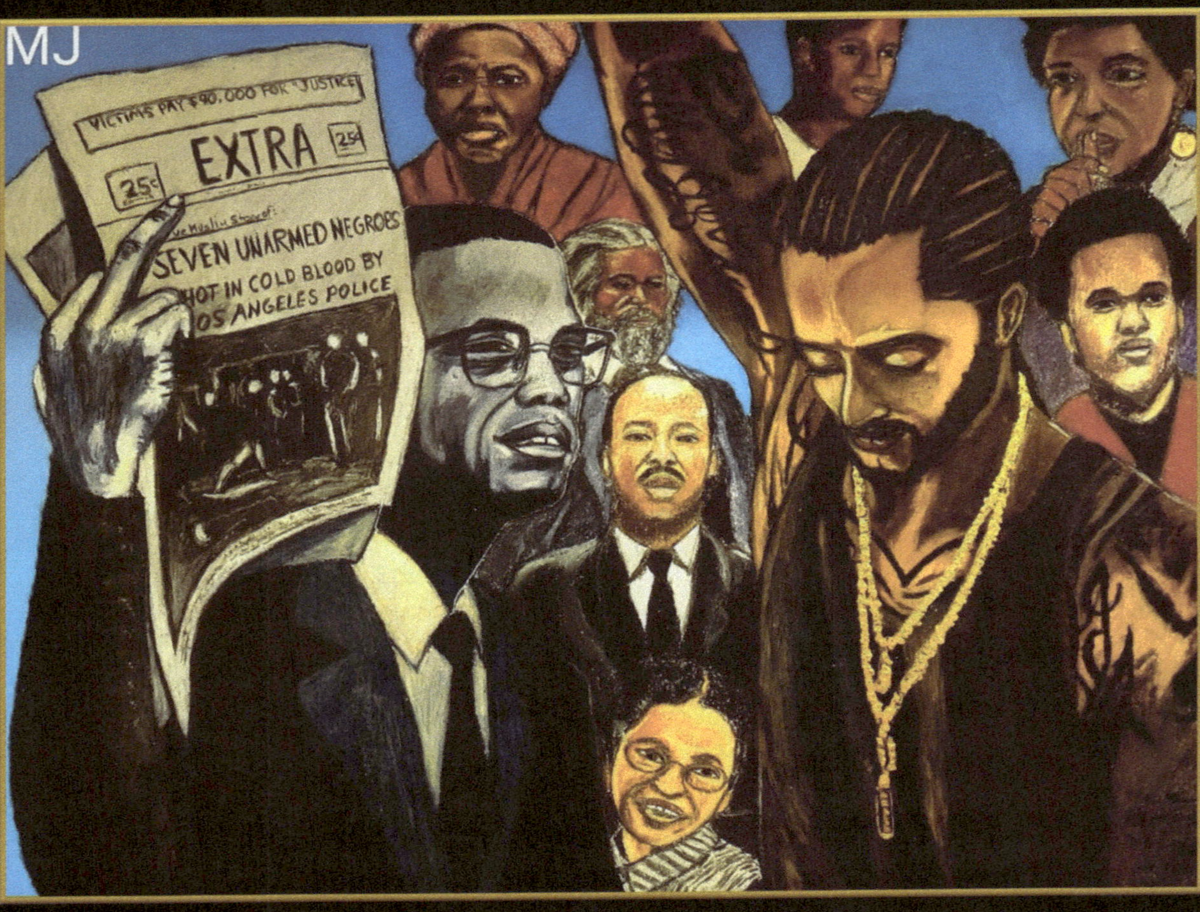

<u>2018</u>

Colored pencils, pastels, and acrylic paint on canvas.

In this drawing/painting, I wanted to pay homage to black activists from past to present who have spent their lives fighting for equality among other things for black people. The process started in 2017 and I finally competed it in 2018. I retouched it a little bit more in 2020. Sometimes a painting or drawing is never fully finished.

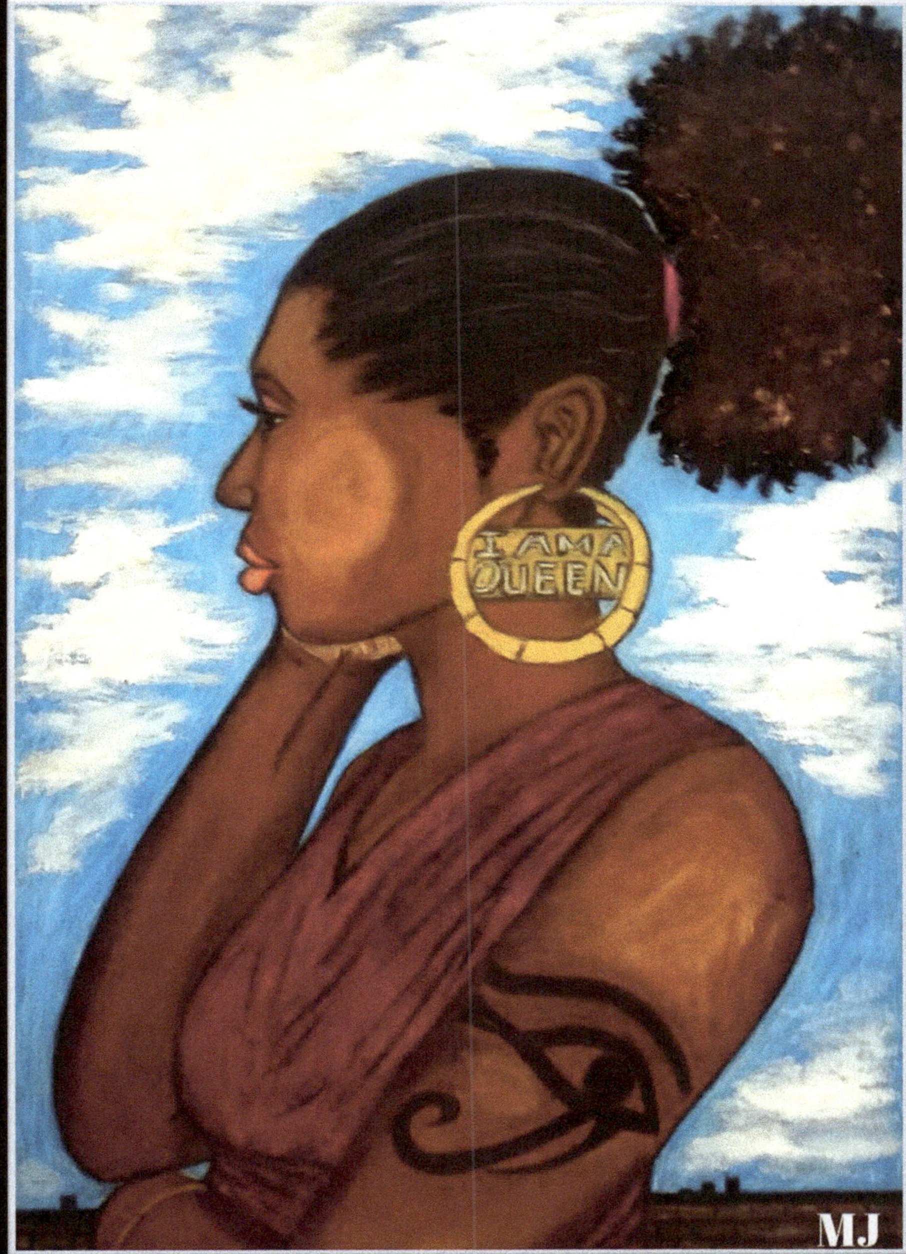

<u>2019</u>

*Colored pencils, oil pastels,
and acrylic paint on paper*

*Made from my imagination, I
created this portrait of a black
woman just chilling on the rooftop
of her building in Harlem looking at
the skyline. I gave her a large
bangle gold earring with the words,
I Am a Queen, embezzled in the
inside.*

*As an artist promoting black love, I
find it important that I push positive
images of black women and black
men as much as possible.*

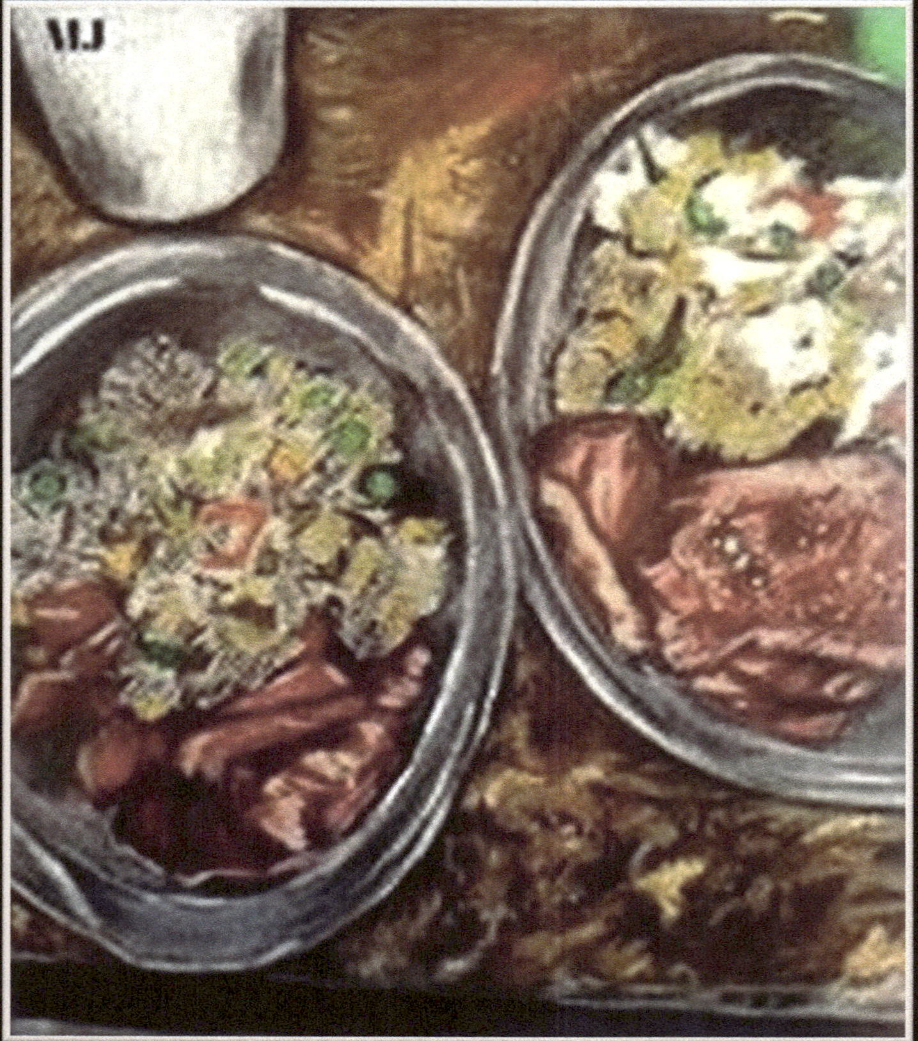

2019

Colored pencils and oil pastels on canvas.

This drawing/painting means a lot to me. It was done as a tribute to my grandmother who suffered from Alzheimer's and dementia. I was her caretaker and one day I prepared a meal containing ham, peas, and rice for her and I to enjoy, which would up being one of her last meals. This was my way of remembering my grandmother and never forgetting the experience that had such an impact in my life.

Portrait of Big Pun

2019

Colored pencils, oil pastels, and oil paint on canvas.

11x14

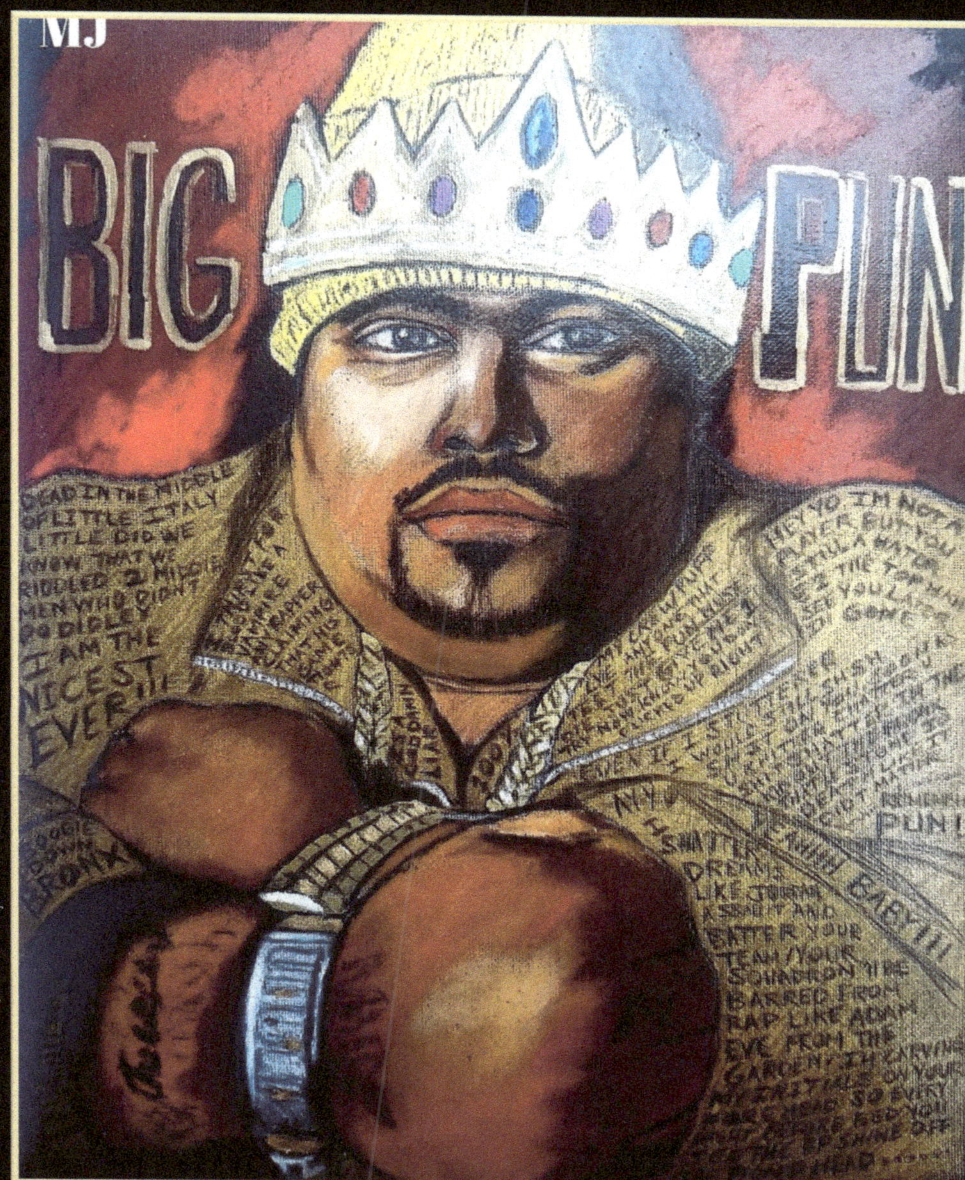

As a huge fan of hip-hop emcee, Big Pun, I wanted to make this a good tribute.

I have done many portraits of Big Pun, but this one I believe is my best. On his shirt are all his well-known lyrics and phrases. On his head is a crown because in my opinion he was just as good a rapper as Notorious BIG.

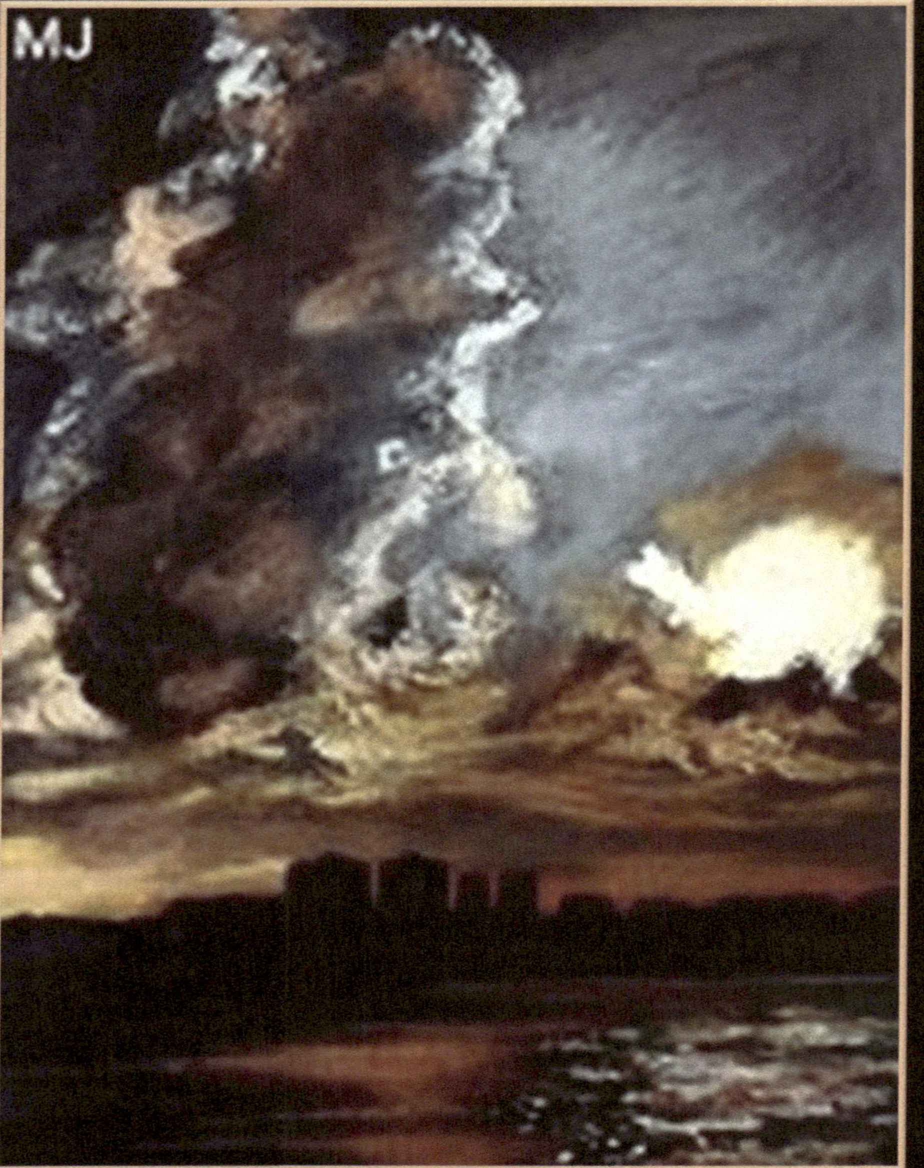

<u>2019</u>

Colored pencils, oil pastels, and acrylic paint on canvas. 11x14

This painting/drawing was inspired by a photo I took many years ago. I drew and painted this natural landscape scene of a sunset sitting above the New Jersey skyline and the Hudson River to display my love for sunsets.

A little Glimpse of Heaven

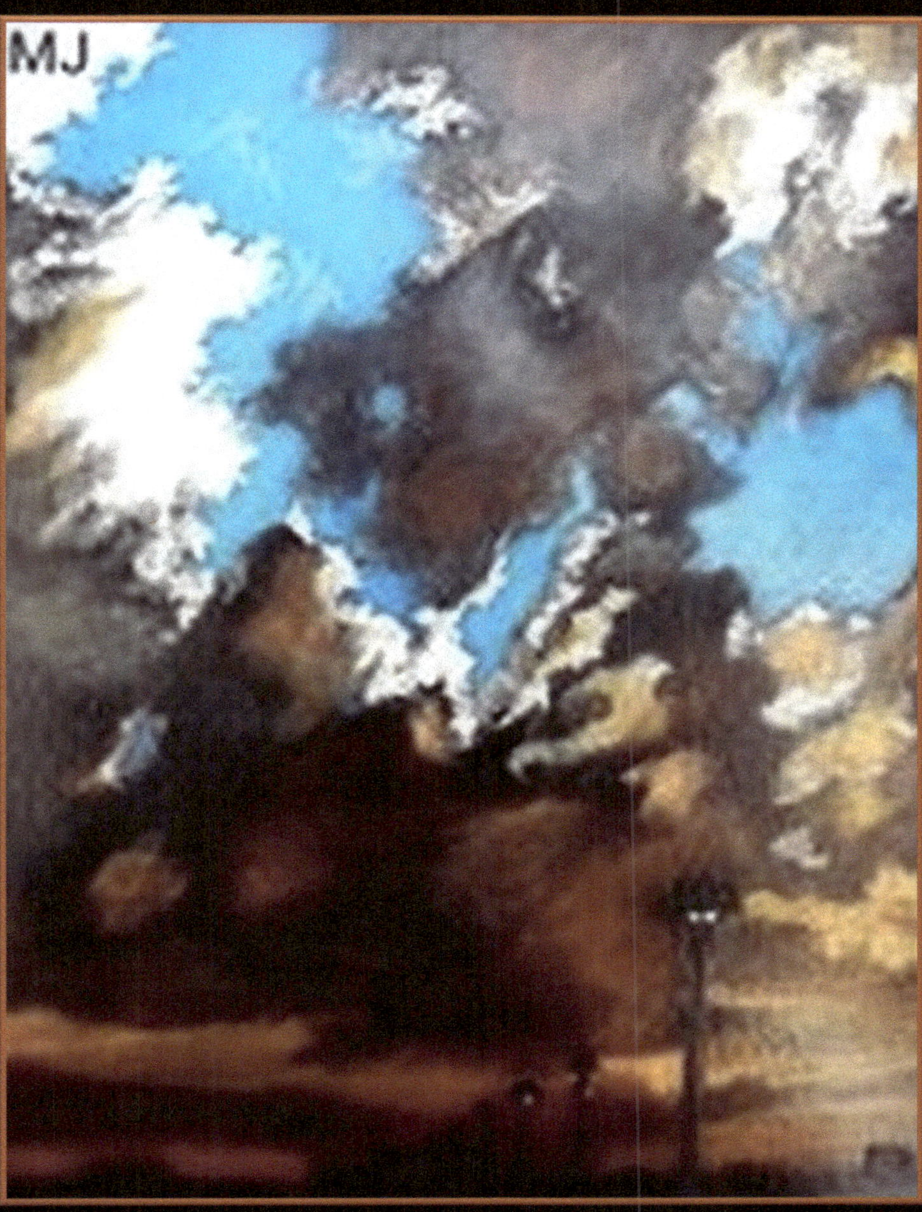

2019

Colored pencils, oils pastels and acrylic paint on Canvas. 11x14

This is another beautiful outdoor scene of a sunset over the New Jersey skyline.

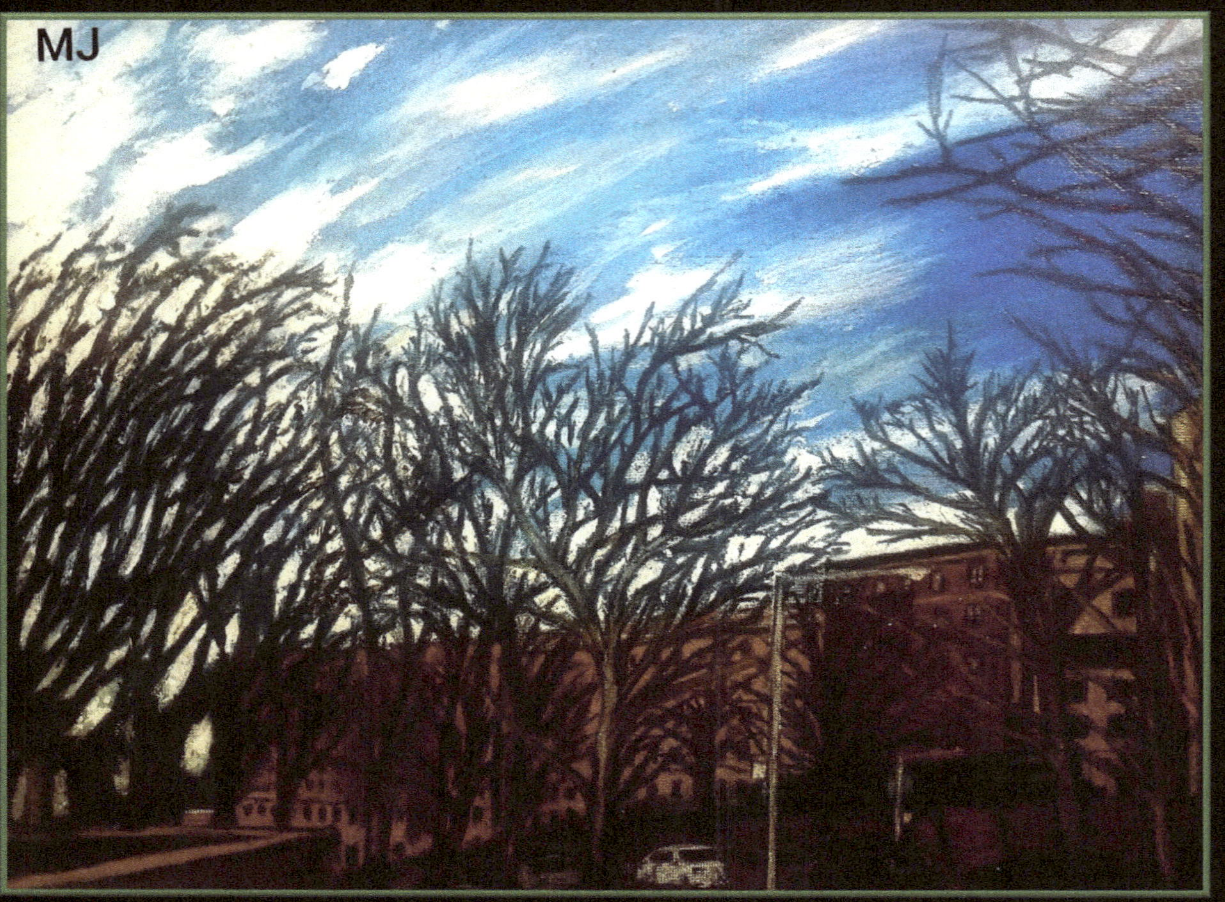

<u>2019</u>

Colored pencils, oil pastels, and acrylic paint on canvas.
11x14

I drew and painted this scene of 150th St. Riverside Drive inspired by an actual photo that I took.

Portrait of Nipsey Hussle

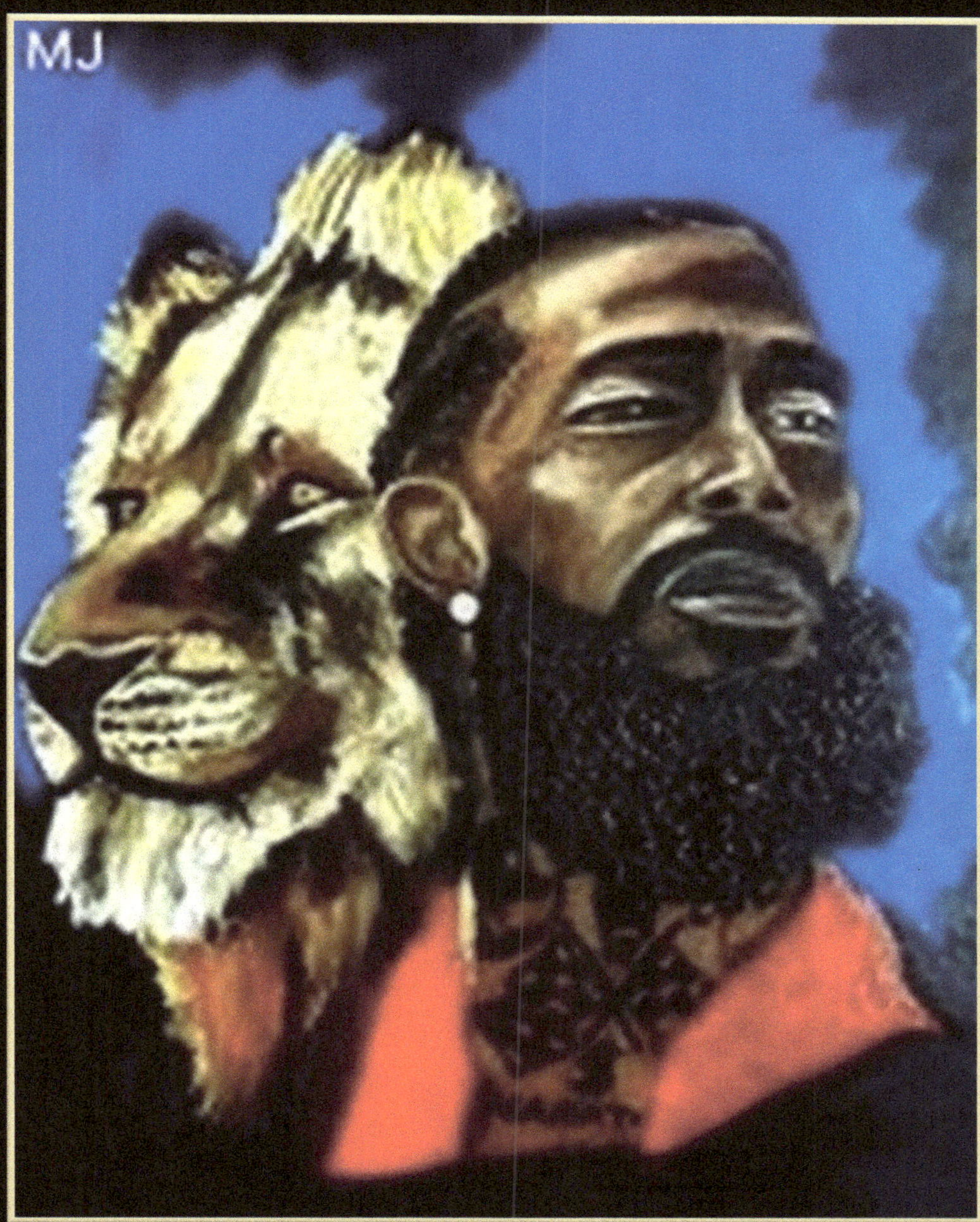

2019

Colored pencils, oil pastels, oil, and acrylic paint.

11x14

Although I wasn't a huge listener of Nipsey Hussle's music, I highly respected the fact that he gave back to his community in LA. He wanted to bring wealth, education, encourage and teach the upcoming youth to be entrepreneurs. I created this portrait of him some days before his would have been 34th birthday.

During the process, I attached Nipsey's head to a lion to symbolize that he was not only a Leo but a leader.

Breathtaking

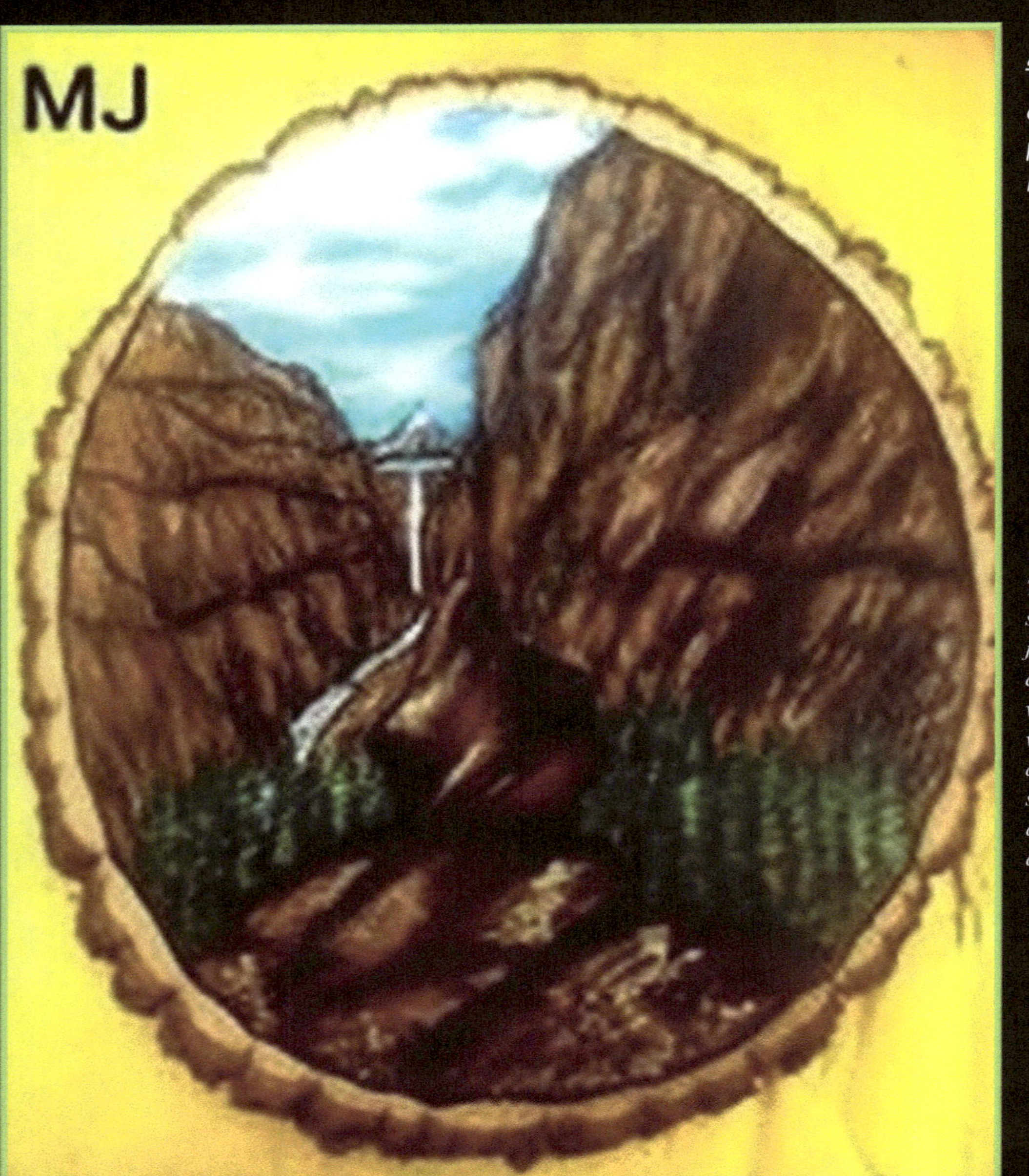

This beautiful nature scene was done as I was just learning how to draw and paint on wooden log slices. I wanted to redo a drawing that me and my sister (who is also artistic) did when I was a kid.

During the process of drawing this scene I wanted the viewer to visualize him or herself as a bird flying over the canyon.

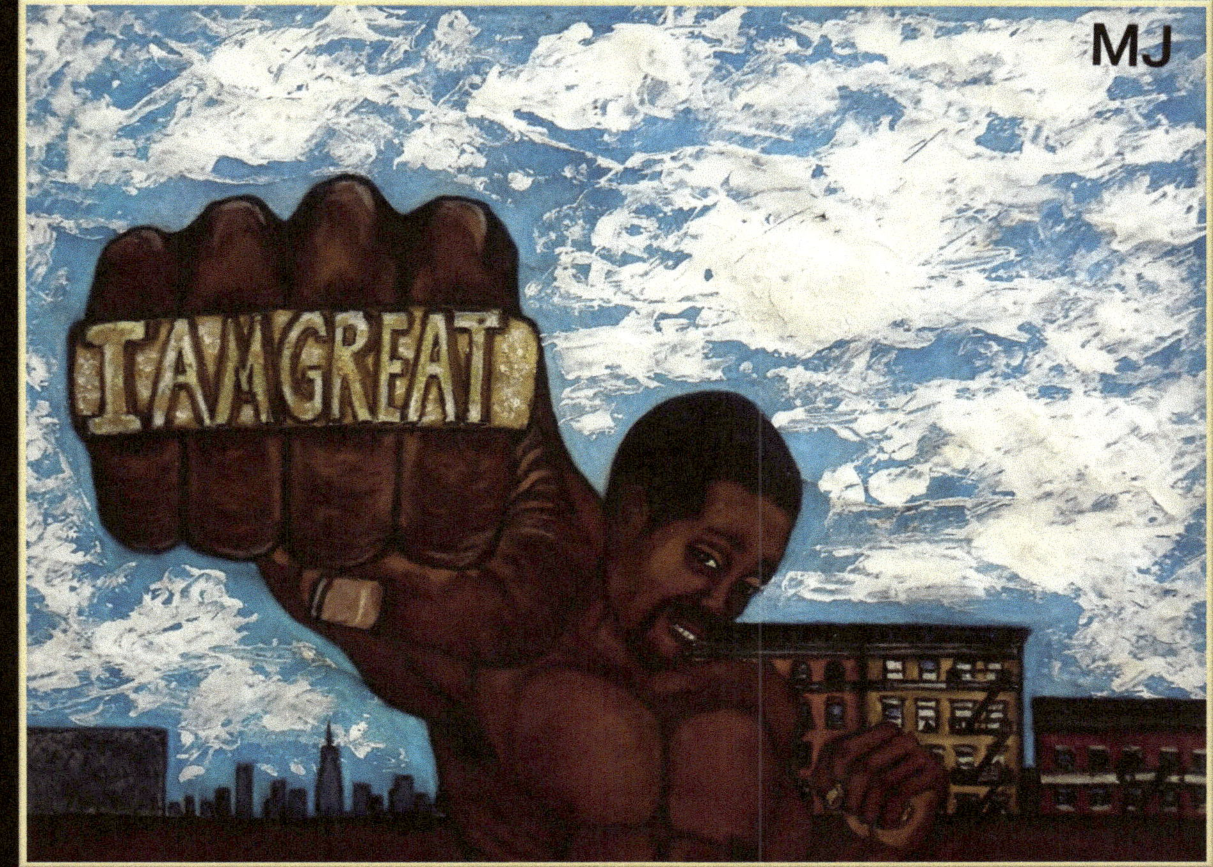

<u>2019</u>

Acrylic paint, oil pastels and colored pencils on paper

This is by far my most personal work of art to date. It deals with overcoming depression and learning to embrace self-love. I started creating this painting originally in October 2019, right after overcoming my darkest bout with depression and realizing the importance of loving myself and not depending on love from someone else. Also, I realized the importance of giving myself positive words of affirmation because sometimes our mind can be our worse enemy.

In the painting a black man puts his hand into a fist forward to the eyes view to show a gold finger ring that spells, I Am Great. I gave it this title to remind myself to always think of these three words whenever I feel discouraged.

Colored pencils, pastels, acrylic paint, and oil paint.

In 2019, novelist, editor, and professor, Toni Morrison passed away. Known mostly for her novels; Beloved, Song of Solomon, and The Bluest Eye, Toni played a pivotal role in bringing black literature to the mainstream. Part of it has a lot to do with her being the first black editor for Random House Publishing Company. Also, she used her voice and platform to speak out against racism and the mistreatment of black people.

This portrait that I painted of Toni shows her with her well-known grey locs and behind her is an image of her younger self holding a paper tablet. On it are the names of her most famous novels.

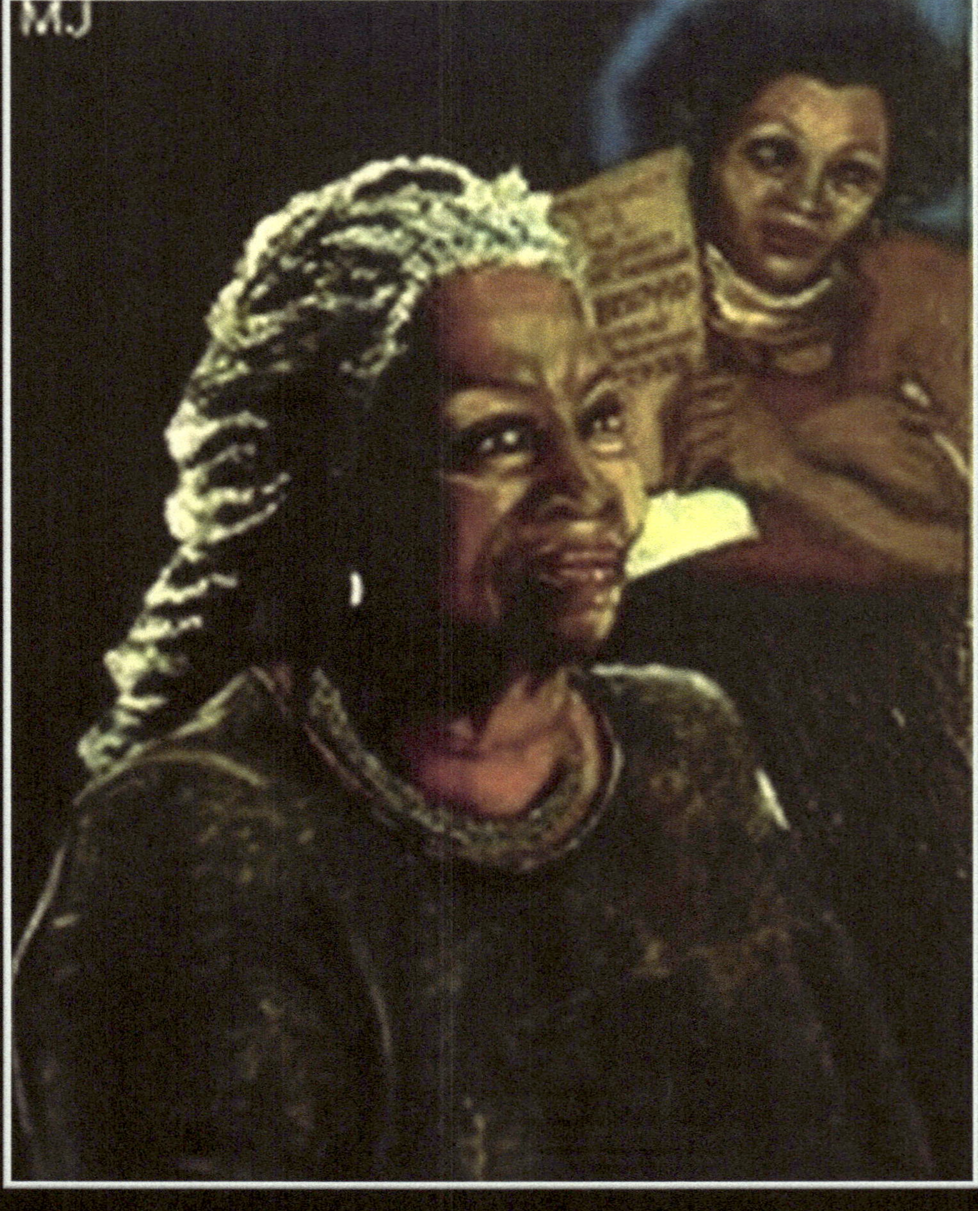

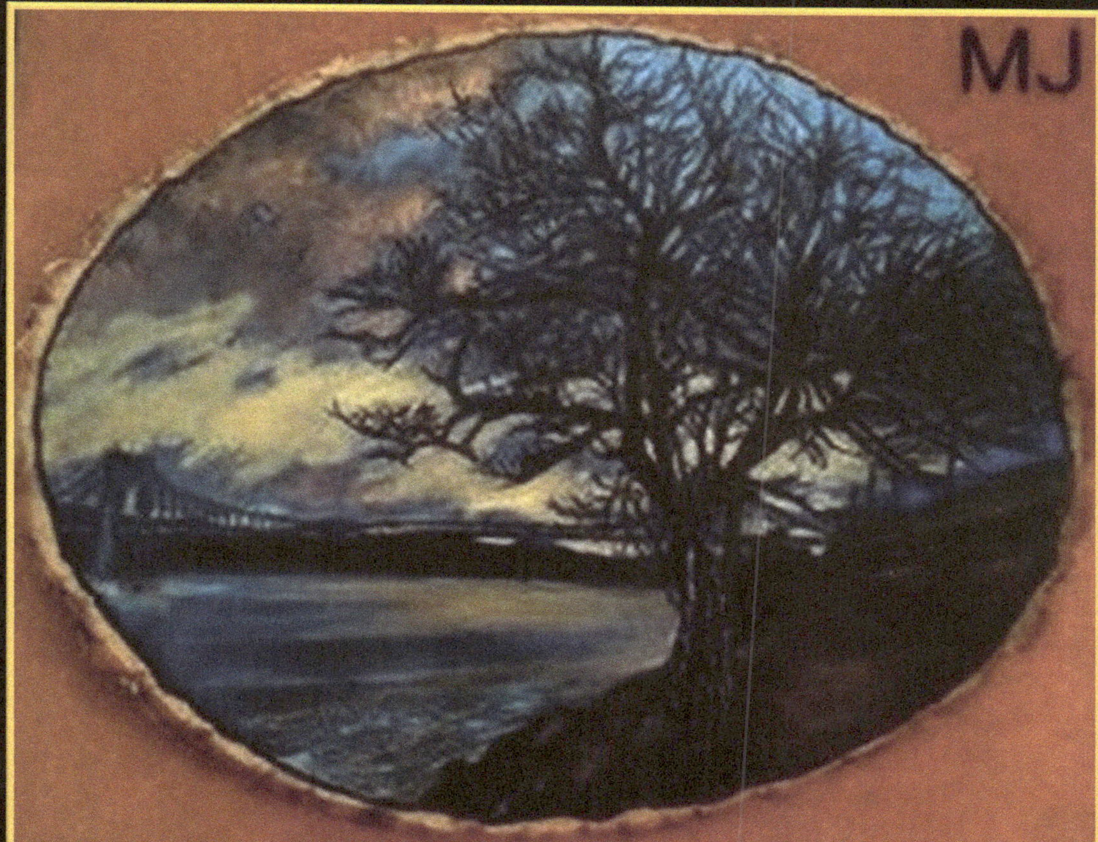

2019

Color pencils,
oil pastels on
wood log slice

*In November
2019, I drew and
painted this
beautiful scene of
a naked tree
standing in front
of the George
Washington
Bridge and the
Hudson River.*

Another Love TKO (Portrait of Teddy Pendergrass)

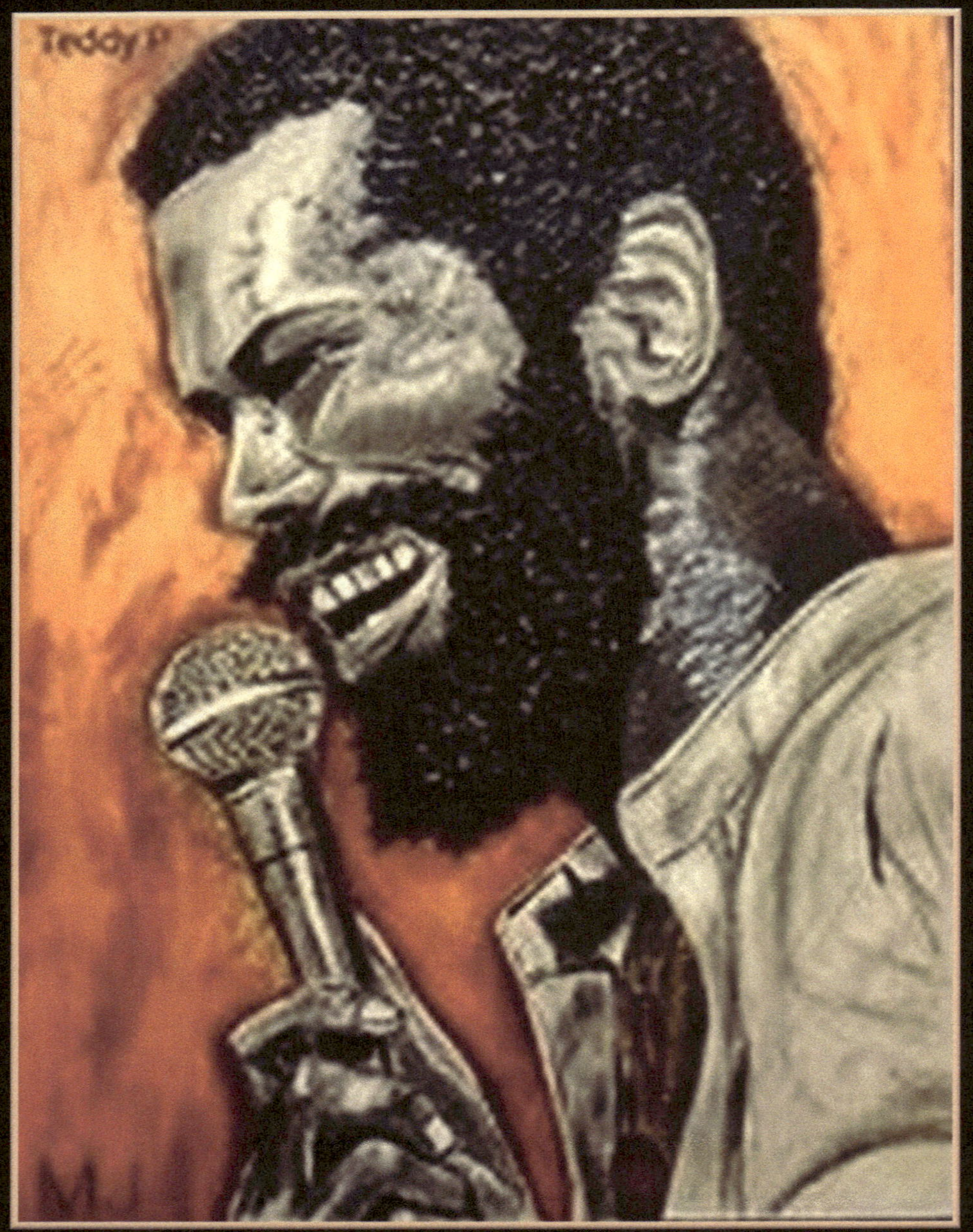

2019

Graphite pencil, charcoal, colored pencil, oil pastels and acrylic paint on paper.

This portrait is of soul singer, Teddy Pendergrass. I first heard of him as lead singer for Harold Melvin and the Blue Notes singing, Wake Up Everybody. The portrait shows him when he was soaring high in his career as a solo artist. I added a lot of texture to his beard and hair to make them appear three dimensional.

Little Ghetto Boy

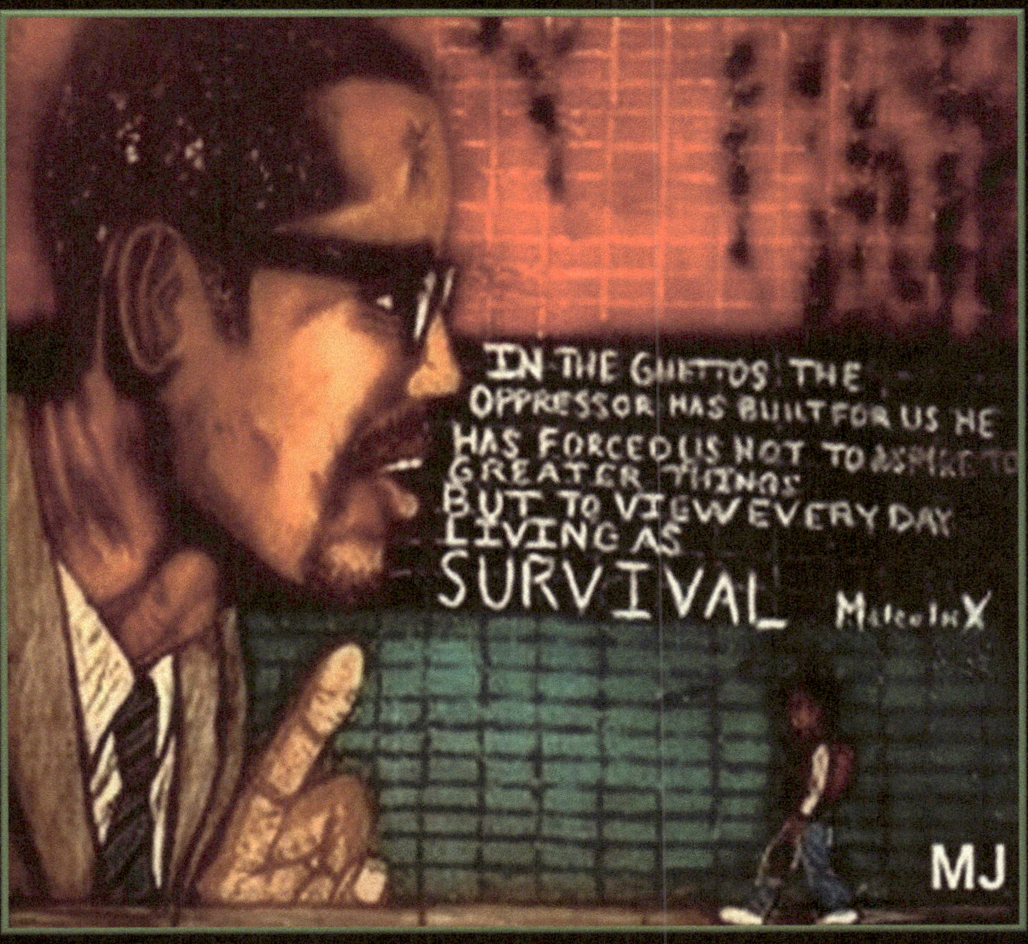

2019

Colored pencils, pastels, and acrylic paint

A famous quote by Malcolm X says, "In the ghettos the white man has built for us, he has forced us not to aspire to greater things but view everyday living as survival. When I heard the quote, I was immediately inspired to create this drawing/painting of a young black boy walking to school. On his journey is a neglected mural of Malcolm X with his famous quote. I titled the painting, Little Ghetto Boy, because I was also thinking of the song of the same name, by the singer, Donny Hathaway.

Black Gold

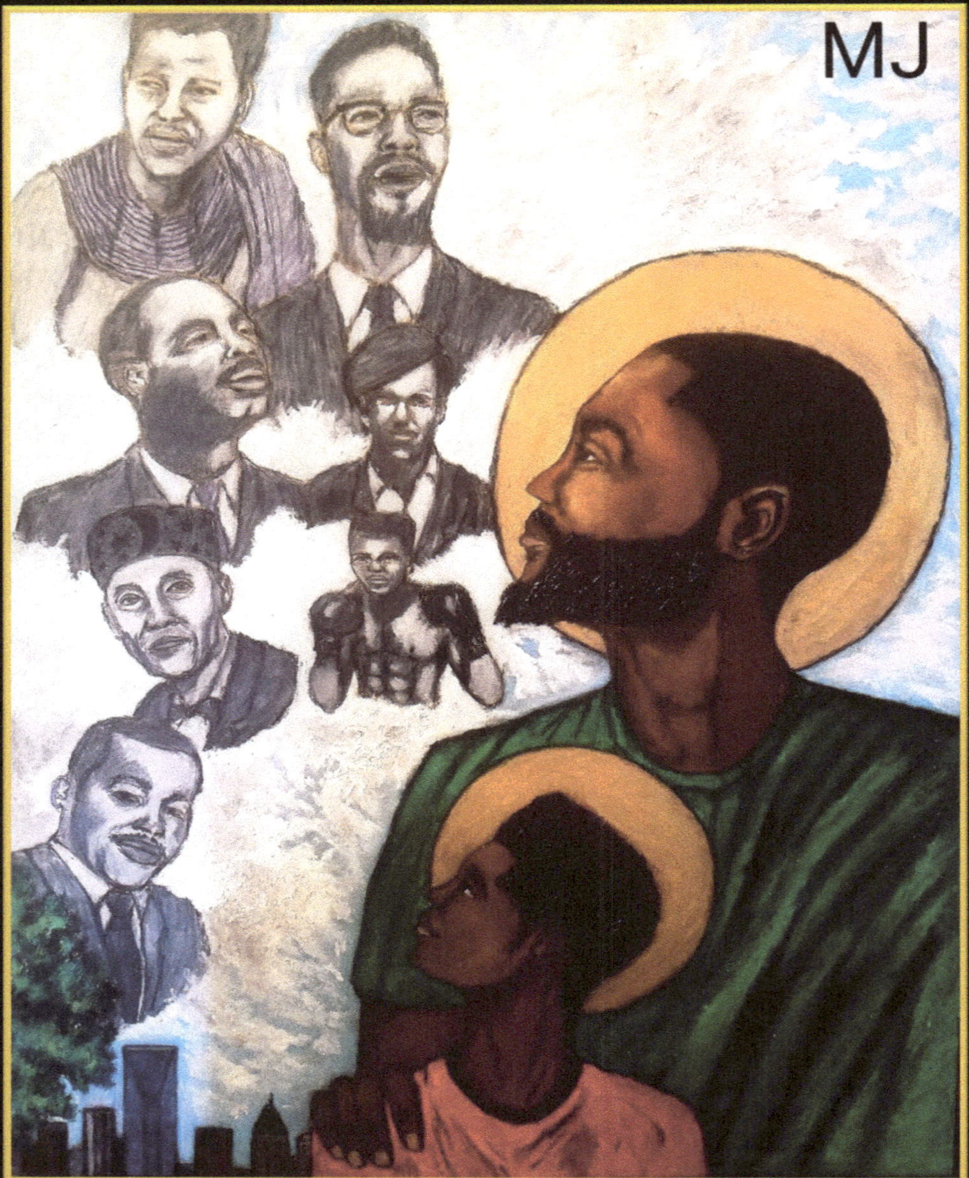

<u>2020</u>

Colored pencils, oil pastels, and acrylic paint on wooden canvas.

This painting is very special to me. Done and completed in the month of February 2020, I titled the piece, Black Gold, inspired by a song of the same name. The song is by singer, Esperanza Spalding, and in the song, she sings words of affirmation and encouragement to uplift black boys and men. Listening to the words touched my heart and left me feeling inspired because there are not too many songs made to uplift black men and boys. I poured my inspiration into this painting. It shows a black man with his son, they are looking up into the sky, and up above in the clouds they see the spirits of great black men before them who made a change for black people. Also, I painted gold circles behind the man and his son to represent the title and to symbolize pride and importance.

2020

*Graphite pencil, and
colored pencil on paper*

*I created this portrait of
Queen Latifah around the
time of her birthday in
March 2020. In the drawing,
Queen Latifah is her
younger self as she poses
with her well-known logo
above her head.*

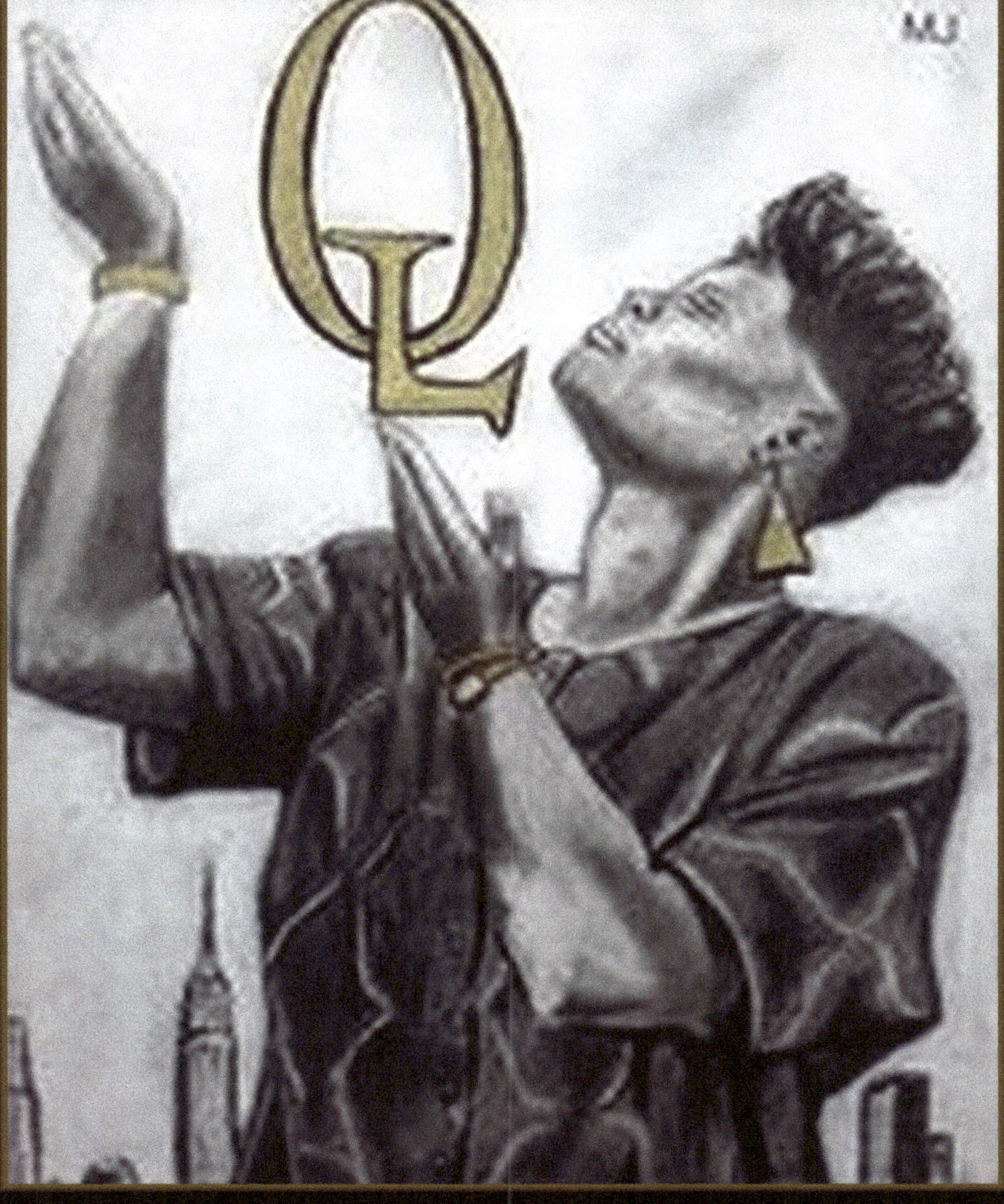

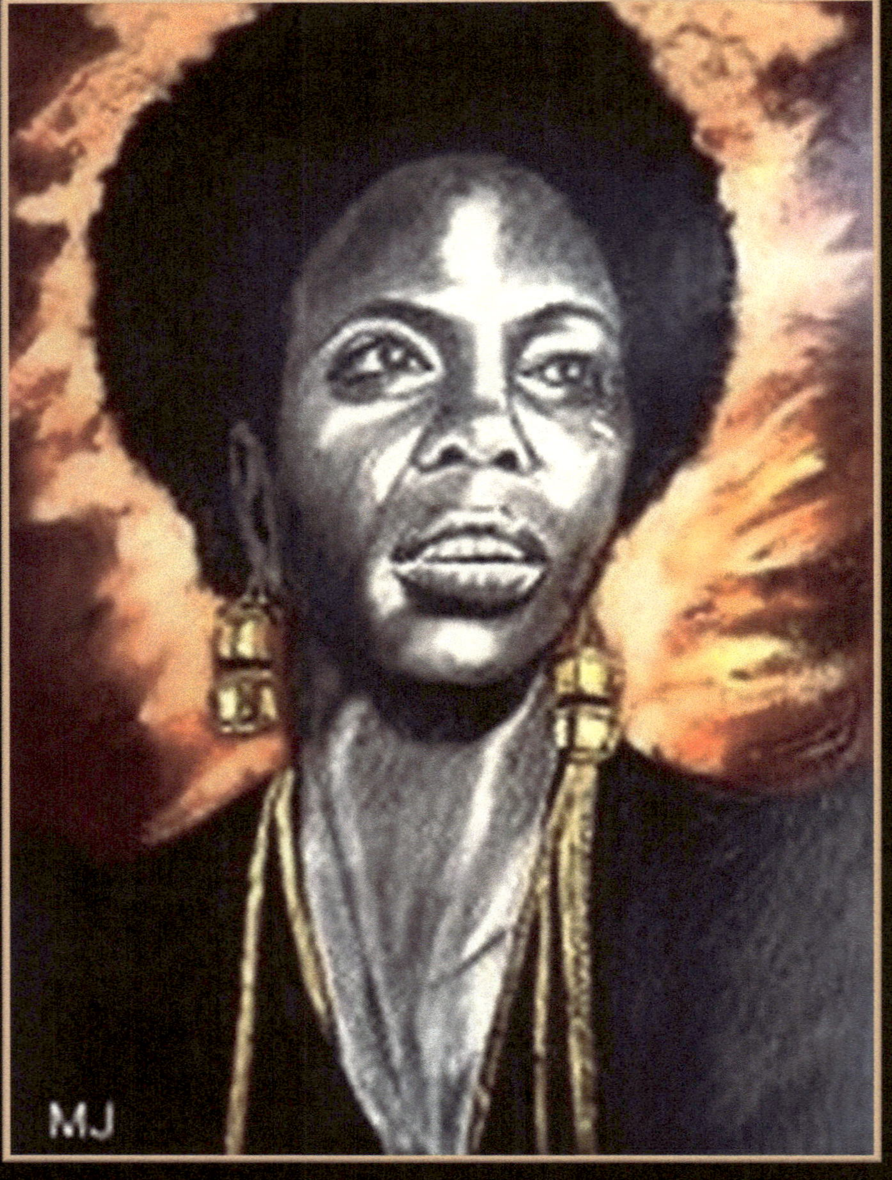

2020

Graphite pencils, oil pastels, and acrylic paint on paper.

I first heard of singer, Nina Simone when I was 18 years old. I had a compilation CD filled with Jazz, Soul, and Blues from the 60s and 70s and one of the songs that I heard was a track called, Black is the Color of my True Loves Hair. I later made it a priority to learn more about Nina and her career. She was a very proud woman who was also proud to be black and she made it her obligation to encourage others like her to be proud of their blackness as well through her music.

This portrait that I drew and painted is a tribute to Nina Simone's memory and her contribution to black music and her voice for activism.

Portrait of Rakim

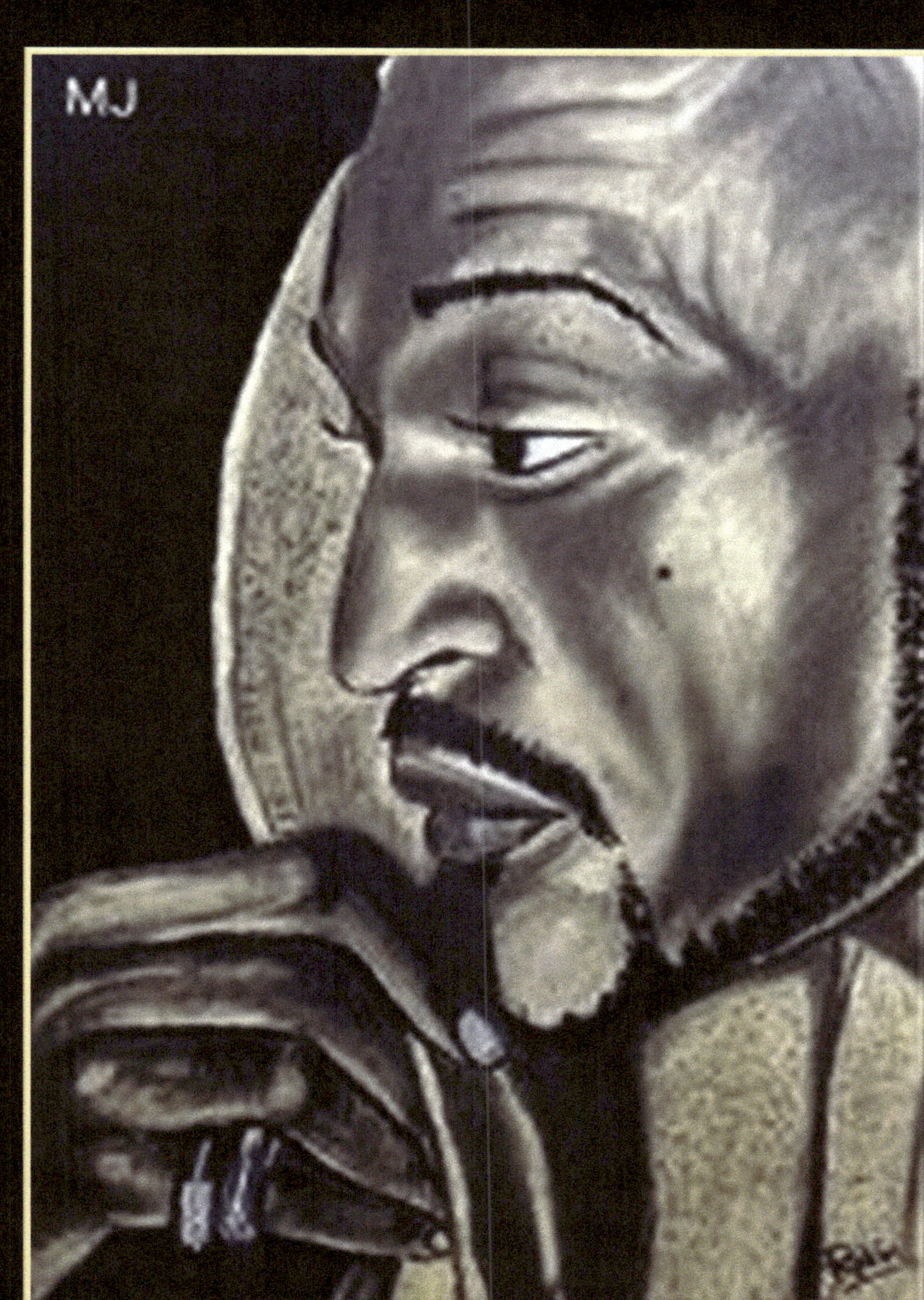

2020

Graphite pencil, colored pencils, and acrylic paint.

I was born in the eighties, when Hip-Hop was still very young. Around 1987 and 1988, I came across an MC by the name of Rakim Allah and his sidekick, DJ Eric B. His lyrical skills at the time sounded so advanced and complex that it forced other rappers to step their lyrical game up. His rhyming inspired a lot of great MCs that came after him. MCs such as Nas for example.

As a fan, through the years, I have created many portraits of him but this one I have to say is my best one as it shows how far I have come in terms of skills in realism.

I created this portrait to honor Sam Cooke who was a very talented singer who was ahead of his time. He didn't just sing; he also wrote songs and even was one of the few black artists who attended to the business side of music by owning his own record label and publishing company. Sam Cooke used his platform to speak out against racial injustice during the civil rights movement.

In the portrait, Sam Cooke is singing on a studio microphone. The dedication is named after his most well-known song, A Change is Gonna Come.

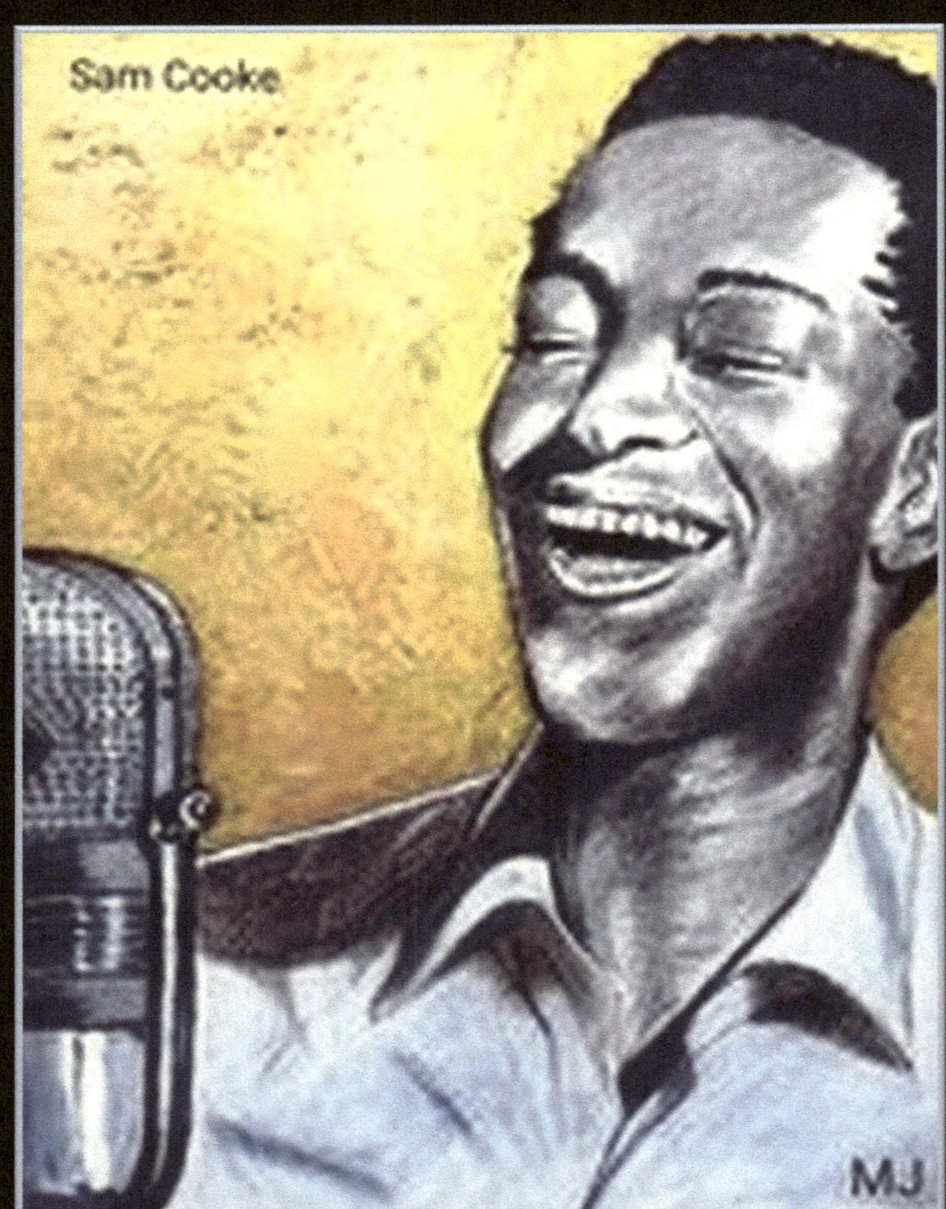

Graphite pencil, charcoal pencil, colored pencil, oil pastels and acrylic paint on paper.

As a huge fan of Hip-Hop duo, Mobb Deep, and being that it was the 25th anniversary of their album, *The Infamous*, I created this portrait as a tribute to their album and as a dedication to the rapper, Prodigy, who unfortunately passed away in 2017.

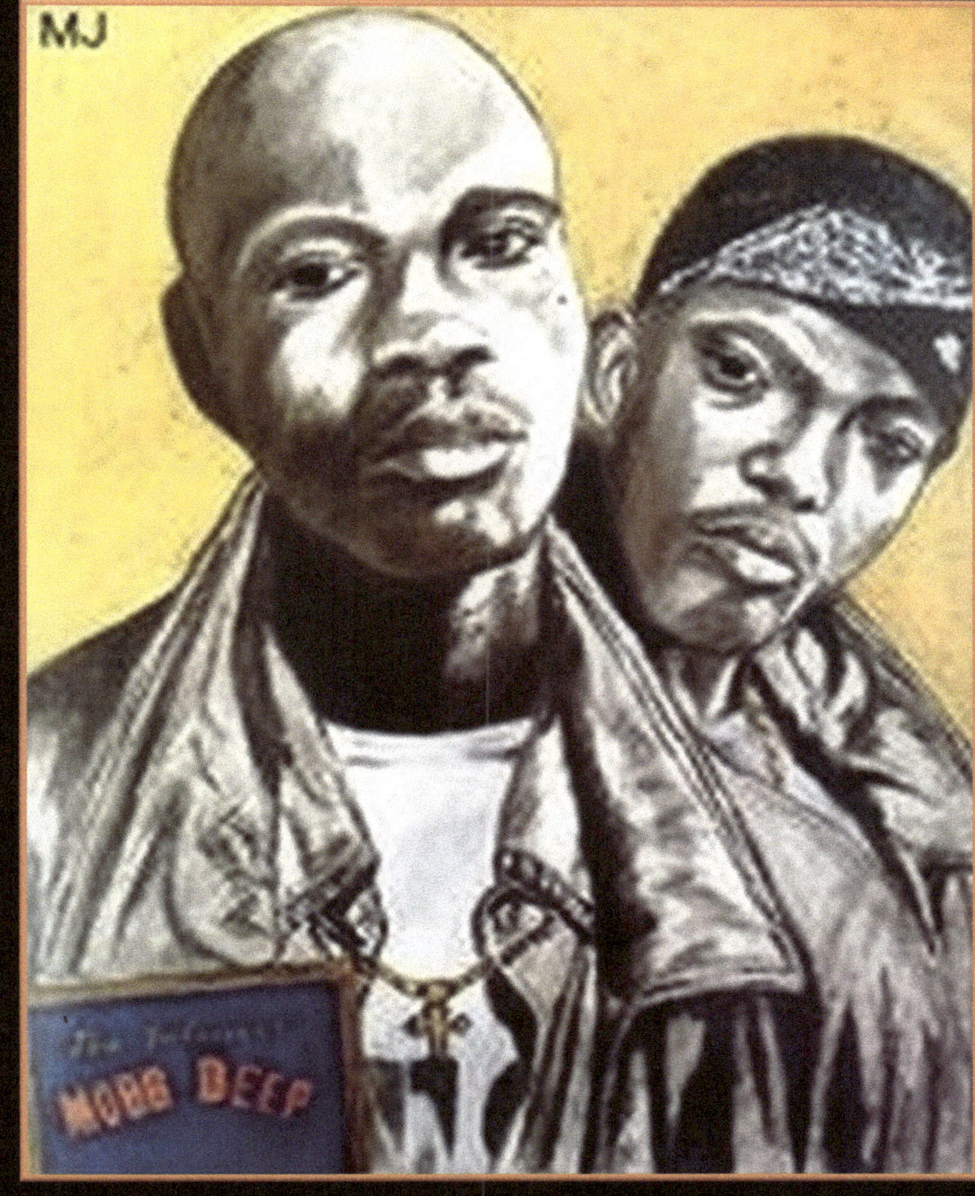

Justice 4 George Floyd

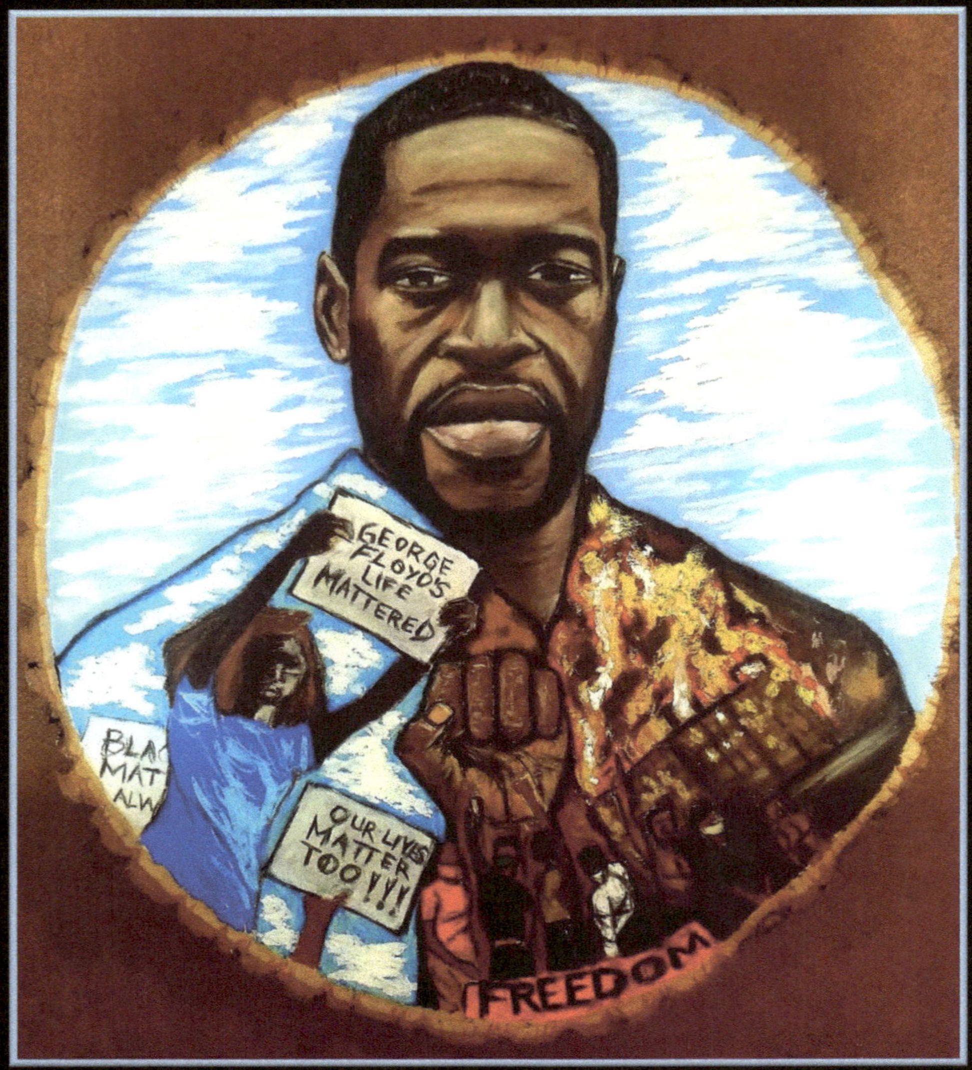

2020

Colored pencils, oil pastels and acrylic on a wooden log slice

This portrait I feel is one of the toughest and yet most important work of art that I have ever created. I am pretty sure that most people will agree that aside from people dying from COVID-19, the worst moment in 2020 was seeing a video of a police officer pressing his entire body weight on the neck of George Floyd. What was done to him was very inhumane, and it outraged the entire world sparking a world-wide revolution.

The portrait shows George Floyd and on his shirt are three pivotal events happening during his protest; a woman holding up a sign that says, George Floyd's Life Mattered. The center shows young protestors passionate about what they stand for and behind is a black fist. The last image shows the precinct that was set ablaze and burned in Minneapolis, Minnesota where George was killed.

Justice 4 Breonna Taylor (Say Her Name)

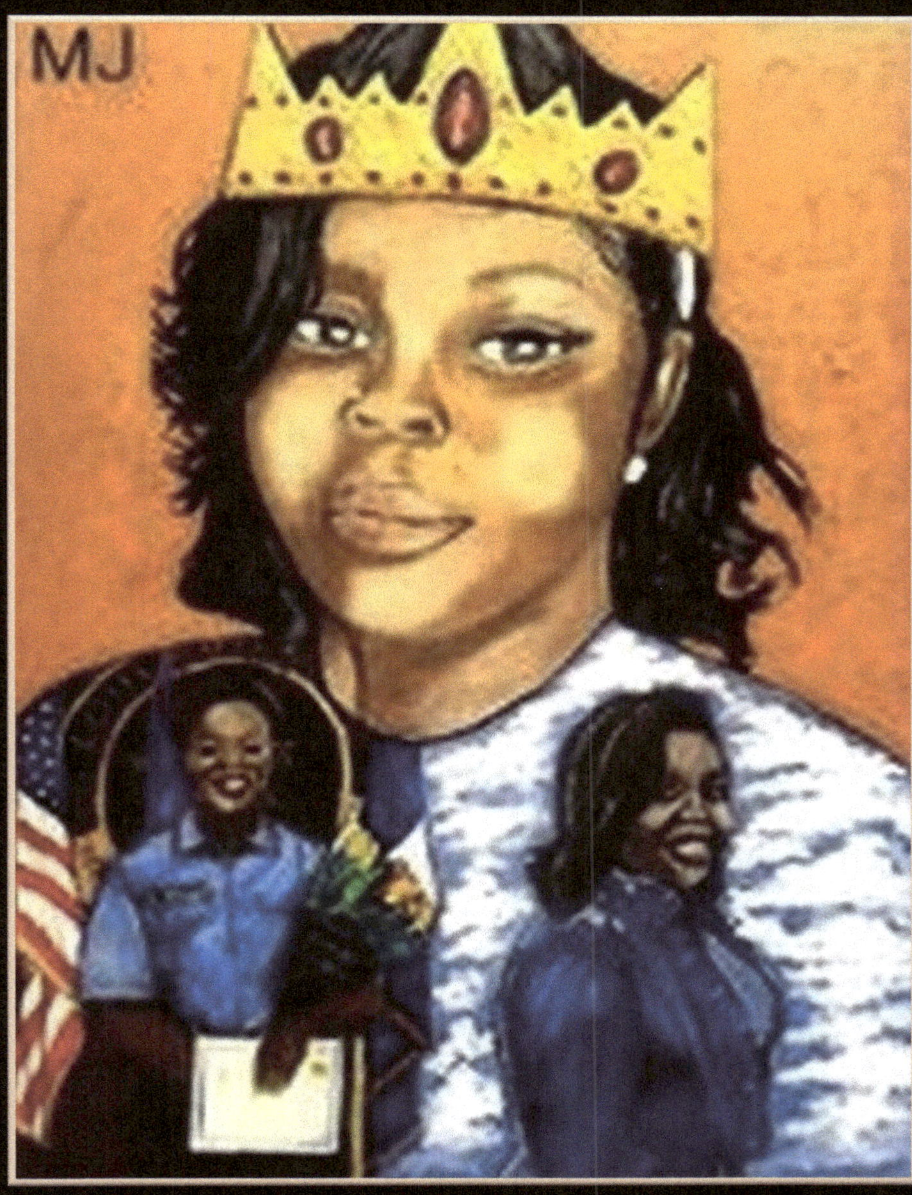

<u>2020</u>

Colored pencils, oil pastels, acrylic paint, and oil paint on wood.

My heart cries out for what happened to this beautiful young black woman named Breonna Taylor who was an EMT technician from Kentucky that was brutally killed by police during an ambush. She was doing good with her life making a difference in her community which makes this tragedy even more sad and unjust. None of the police responsible for her death were found guilty. In this painting tribute, the first image has her with a crown on her head. Inside her shirt are two events in her life; one of her graduating and becoming an EMT and the other of Breonna dressed up and ready to have some fun.

Phenomenal Woman (Portrait of Maya Angelou)

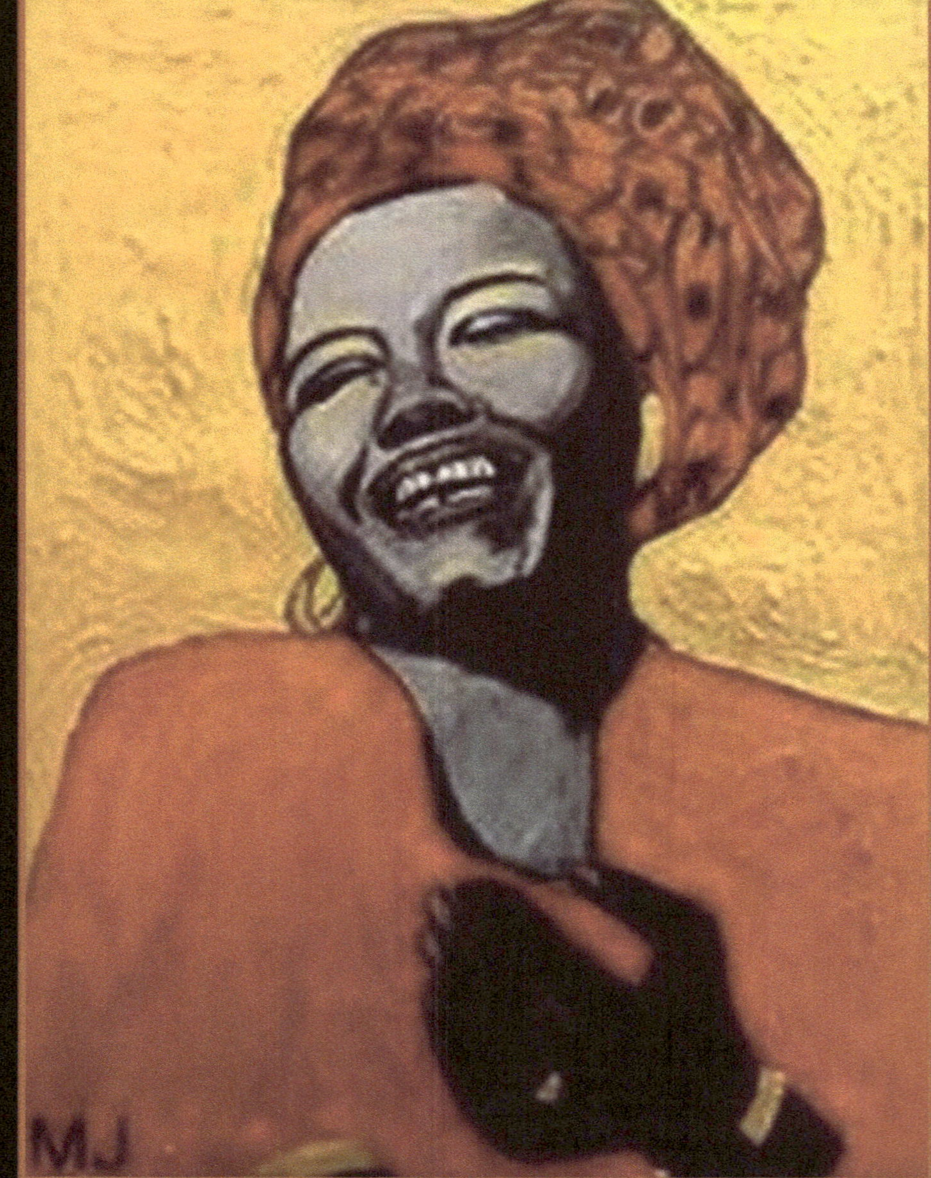

I drew and painted this portrait as a tribute to poet, author, and activist, Maya Angelou. I named the painting after one of her well-known poems, Phenomenal Woman.

Portrait of Rayshard Brooks

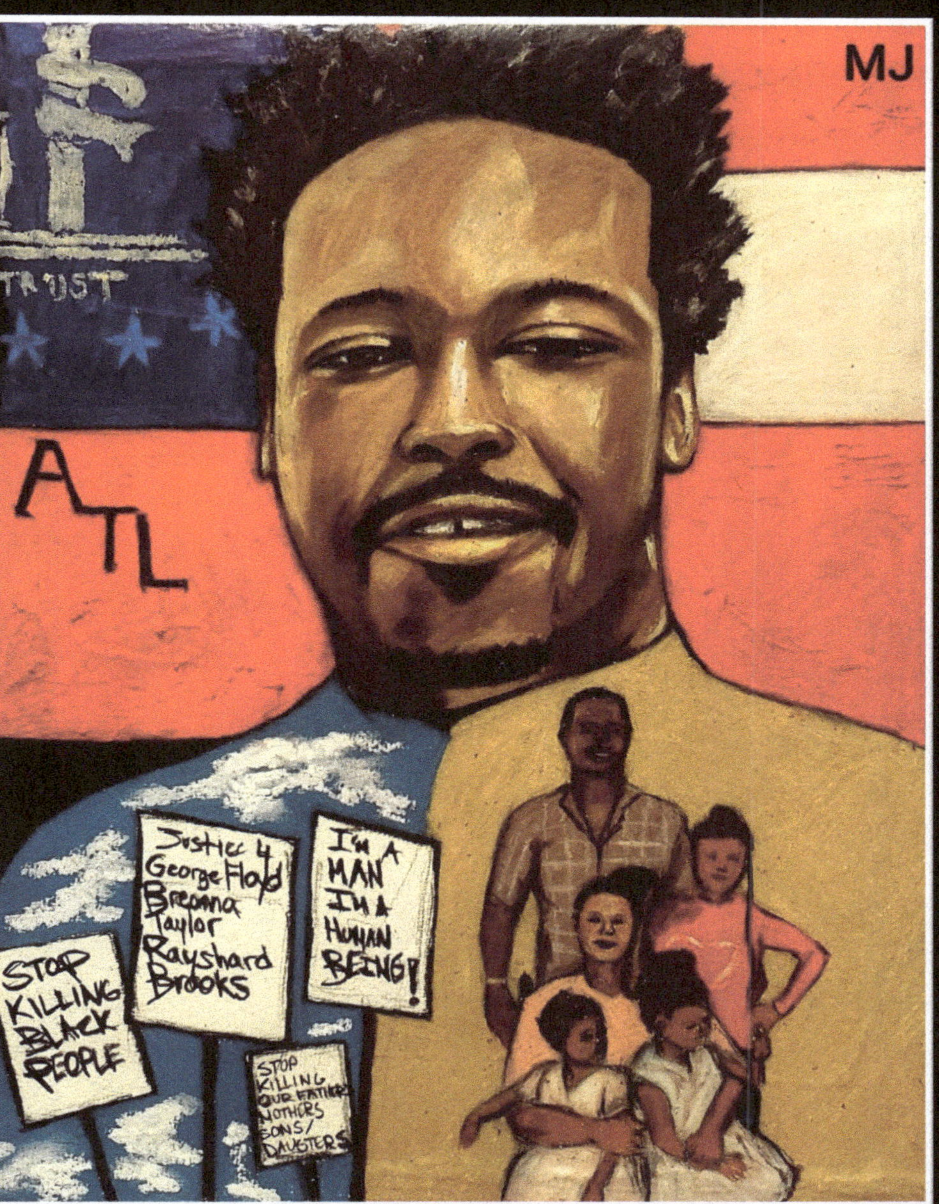

<u>2020</u>

Colored pencils, oil pastels on canvas.

Another sad tragedy that occurred in 2020, the murder of Rayshard Brooks by police in Georgia. I painted this tribute in his memory. It shows Rayshard in front of the state flag of Georgia, while inside of his blazer shows protest signs, one with his name along with the names of George Floyd and Breonna Taylor. On the other side, shows him with his wife and daughters.

Eve (Portrait of Rapsody)

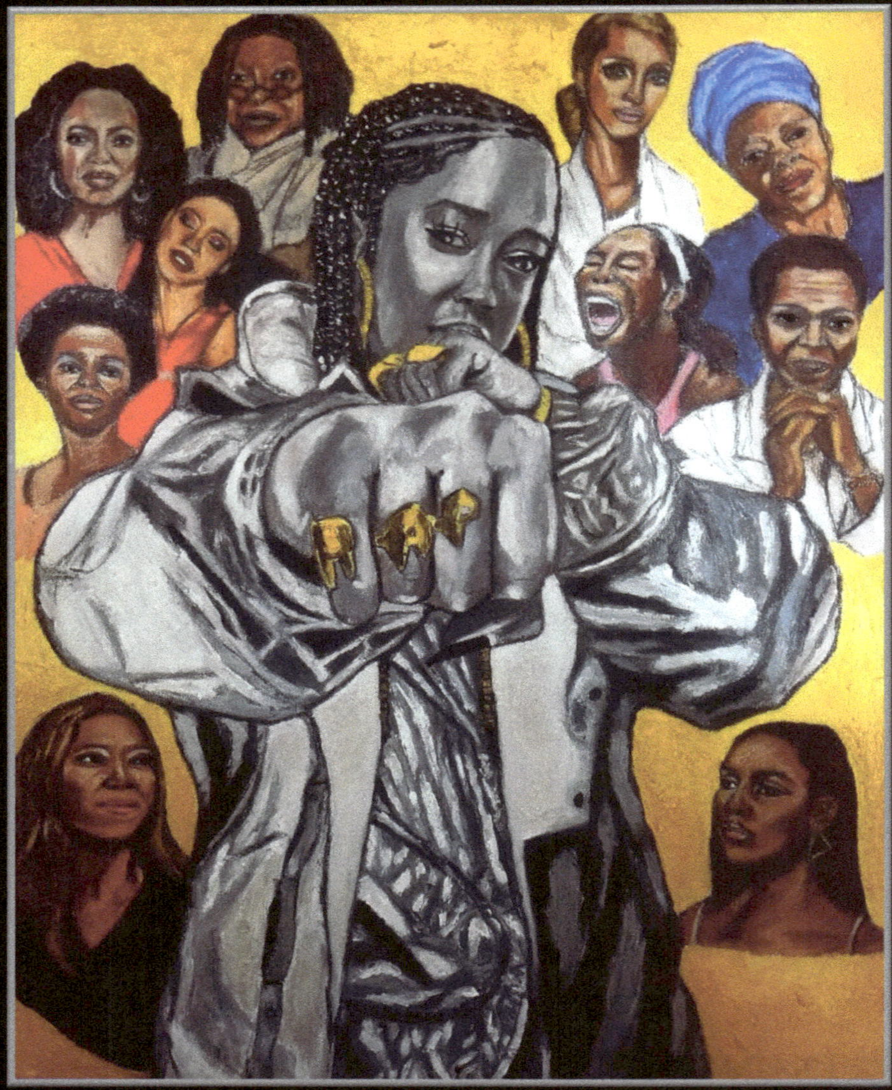

2020
Colored pencils, oil pastels, paint marker, acrylic paint, and oil paint on
wooden canvas.

I would have to say this portrait/painting is the most challenging I've ever done. My aim was to make it appear realistic as possible and to do that I needed to take my time, which took about four plus months. This portrait of rap artist Rapsody is dedicated to her album titled, Eve, which is a celebration of black women. Each song is named after an important black woman (past and present) that has left a mark in history. In the painting, Rapsody is in the center and is surrounded by the faces of the women that she named her songs after. Unfortunately, I did not have enough space for all of them, so I only painted the women of who's names are the titles of my favorite songs. The overall process tested my patience, but it was well worth it. When I showed it on social media and tagged Rapsody, she actually responded and loved it.

Tree Of Pride # 2

<u>*2020*</u>

Colored pencils, oil pastels, and acrylic paint on wood.

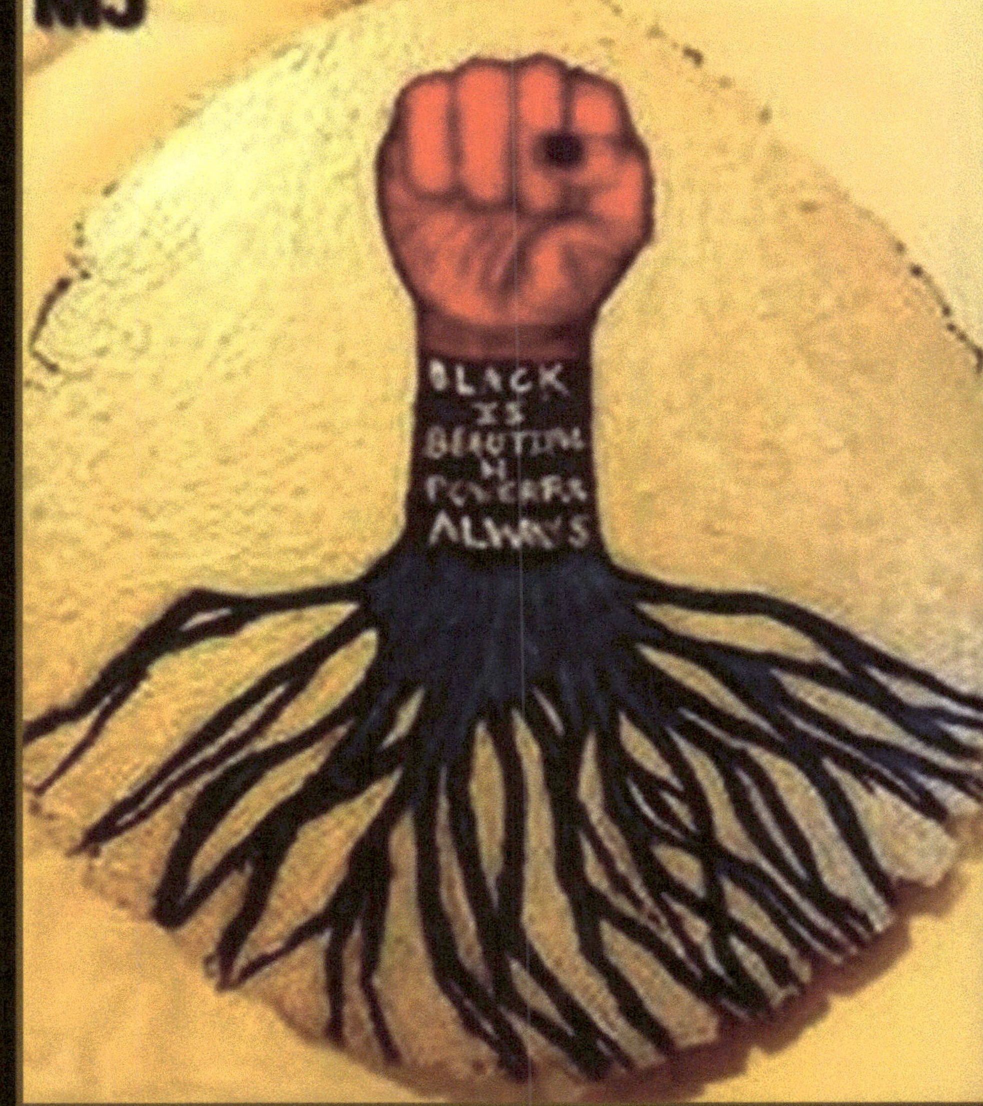

When I created this piece, I thought about my ancestors and all those who were killed at the hands of racists cops or racism. I also created this piece as a response to all the tragedies and protests that occurred in 2020. On the trunk reads, Black is Beautiful and Powerful Always.

Kollage (Portrait of Bahamadia)

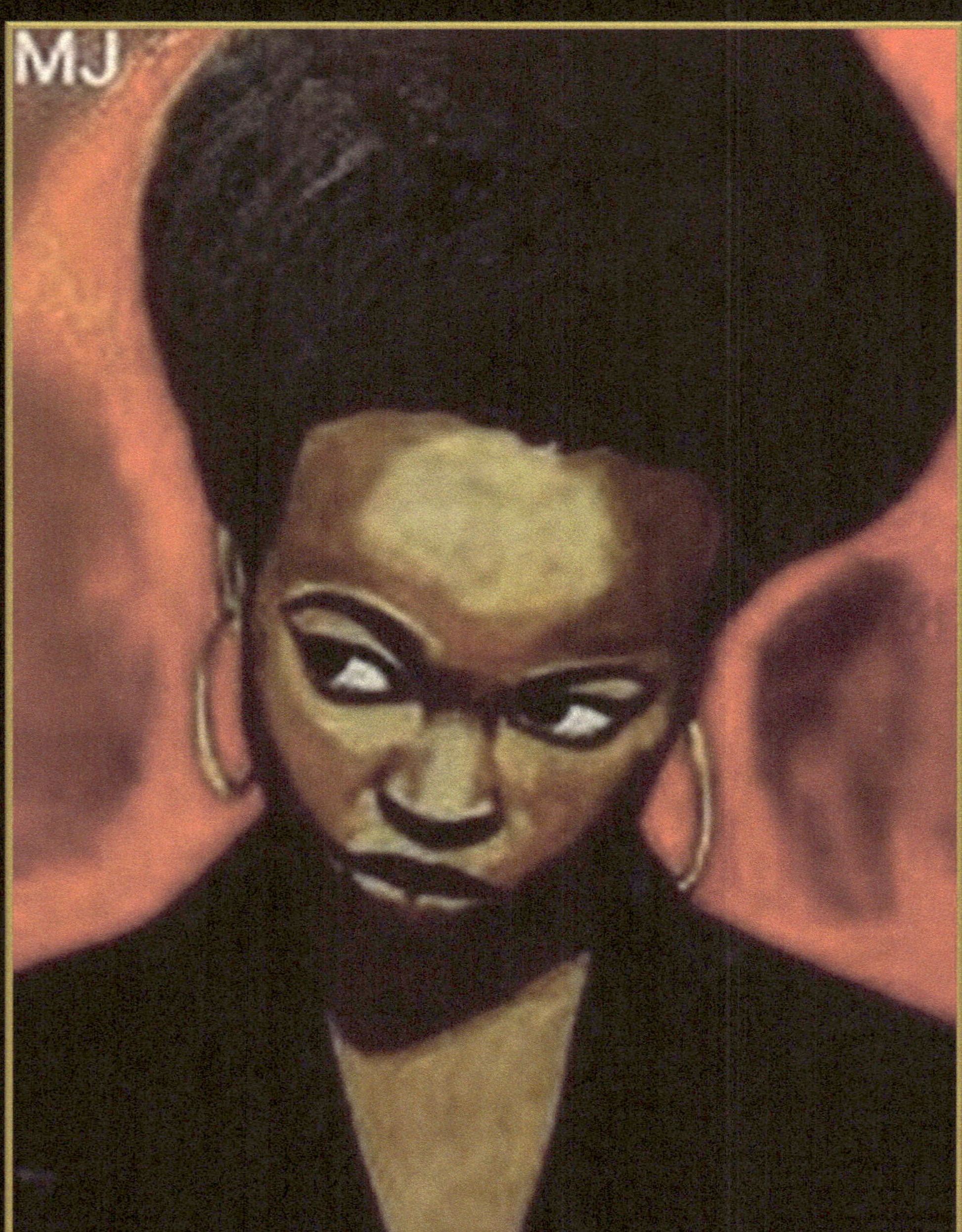

_2020_

Colored pencils, oil
pastels, and acrylic paint
on wooden canvas.

*This portrait is of Philadelphia
rap artist Bahamadia. In 1996,
she came out with her debut
album titled, Kollage. This
painting is a tribute to the
album cover.*

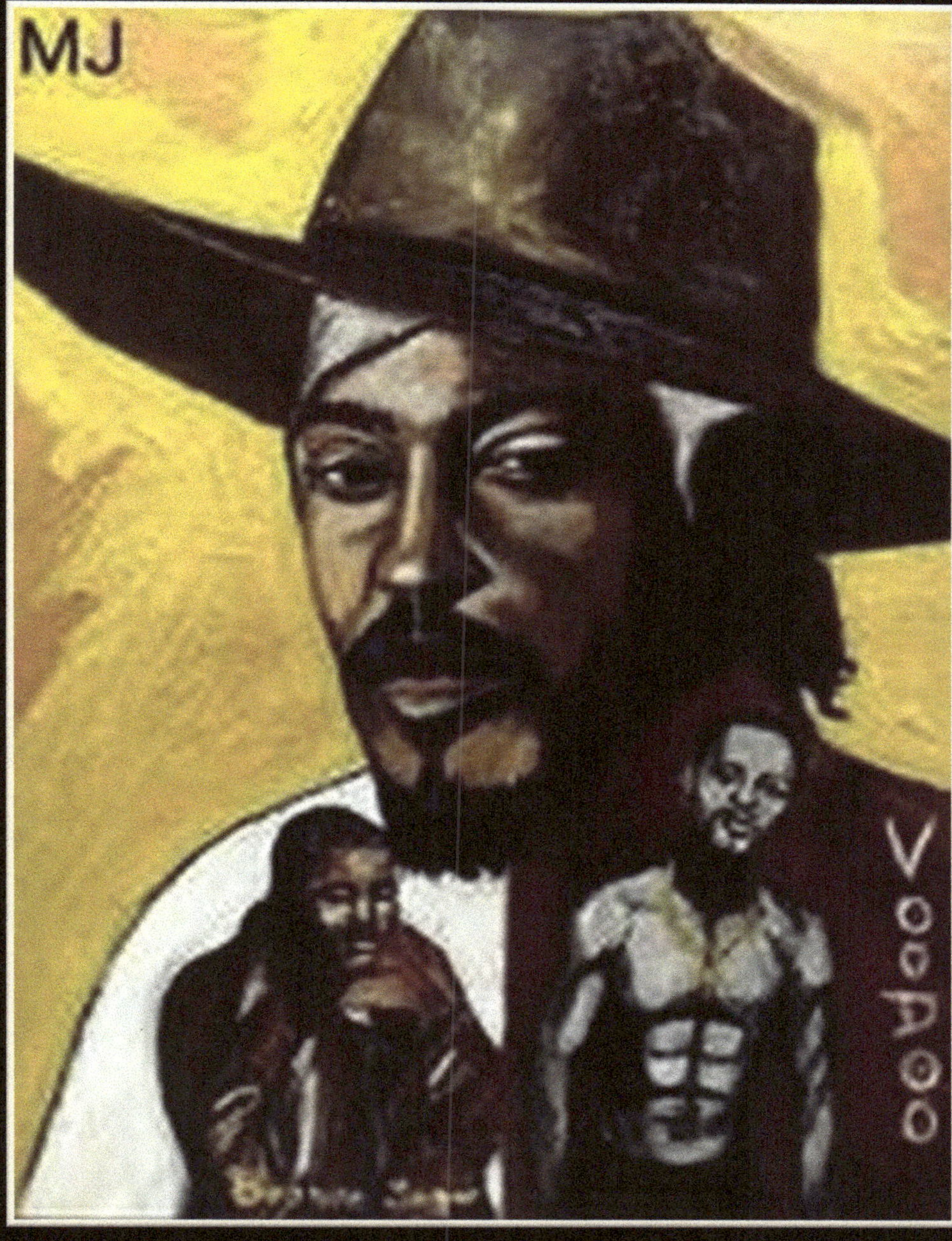

2020

Colored pencil, oil pastels, and acrylic paint on wooden canvas.

The Evolution of D'Angelo is basically a painting that shows the transitions that the soul singer and musician D'Angelo has made throughout his career. From his Brown Sugar stage where the music was mainly jazz influenced, to Voodoo, which was more soul/psychedelic funk influenced to now where his style includes pieces of rock and roll.

Nature In Autumn Series (1)

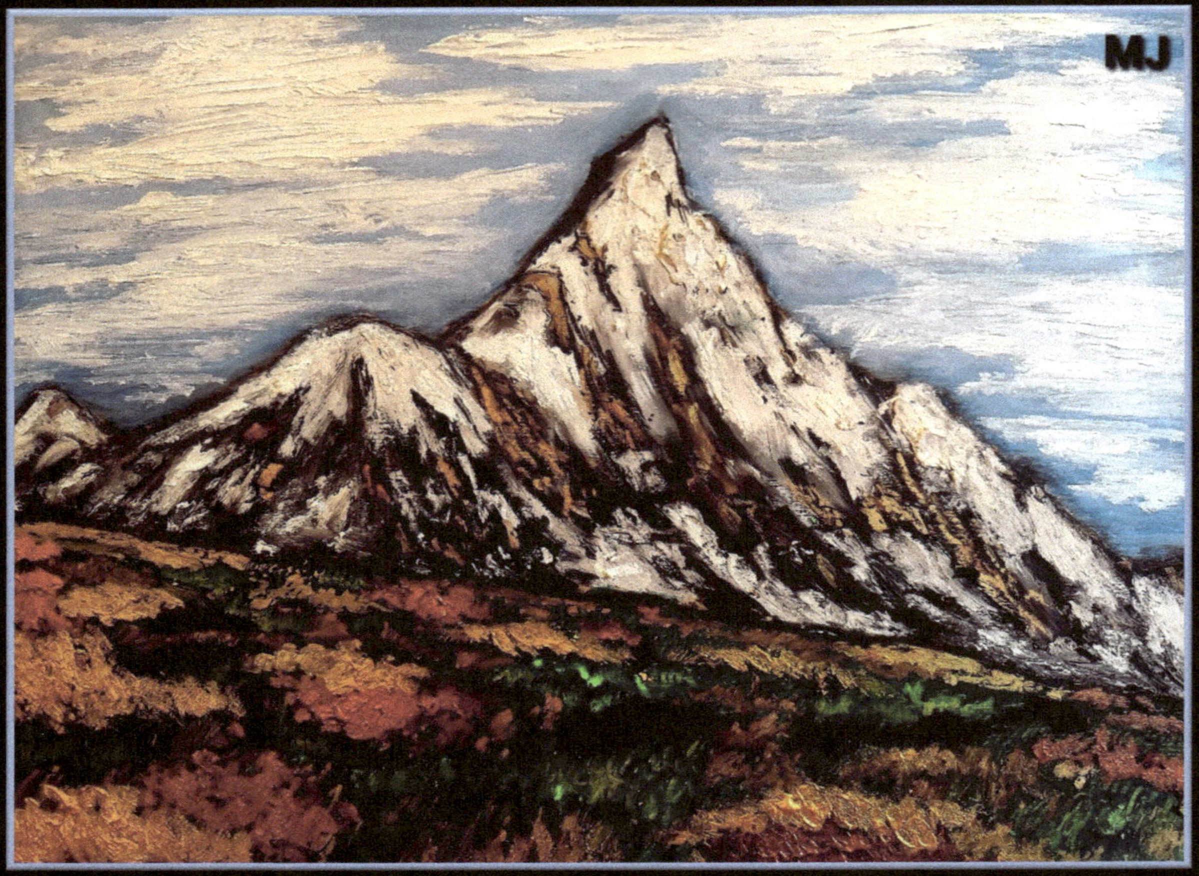

2020

During the fall season of 2020 I decided to create these next 3 paintings of landscape scenes that are related to the season of Autumn. I called the series, Nature in Autumn.

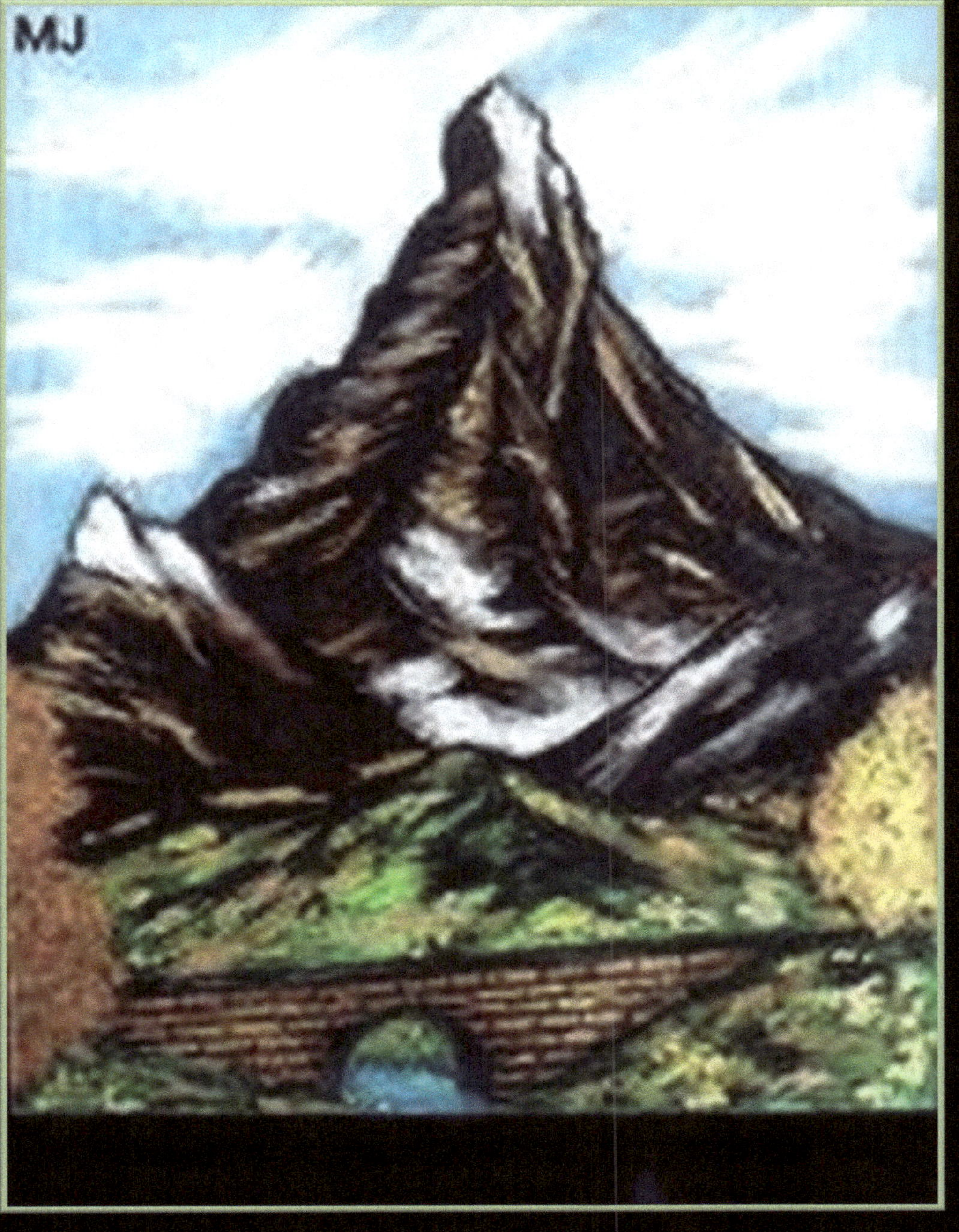

2020

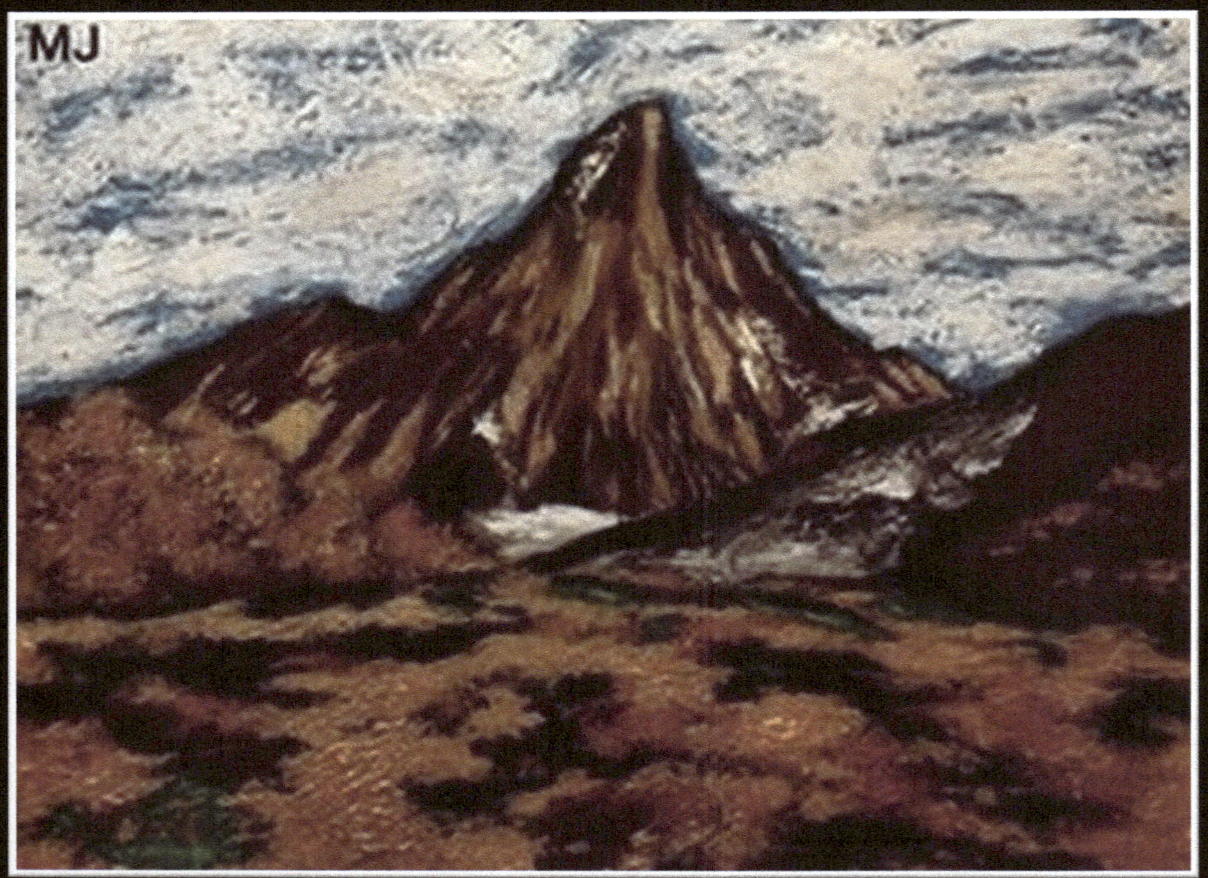

2020

Forever King (Portrait of Chadwick Boseman)

In December of 2020, actor Chadwick Boseman unfortunately lost his life to cancer, which left the world devastated and shocked because we had no idea he was suffering from the disease. Chadwick will always be remembered for his incredible gift as an actor and his love for his culture. Young black kids in America and across the globe gained a new level of self-confidence when Chadwick played King Tchalla aka Black Panther.

In this tribute painting, Chadwick wears Ancestral Planes. Down below shows him in different moments of his life. Behind him is the black panther goddess welcoming him back to the ancestral planes. This painting I feel is some of my best work that I've ever done.

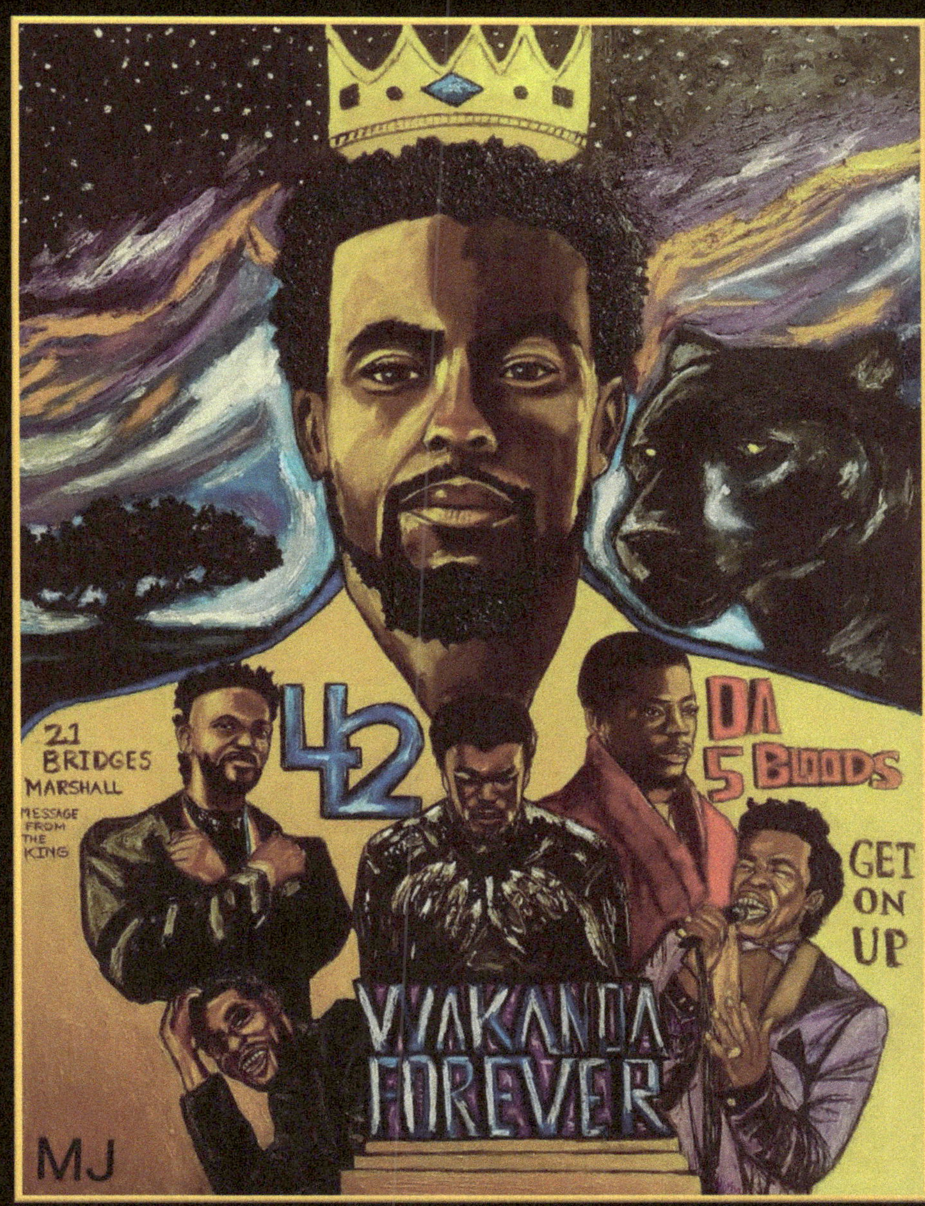

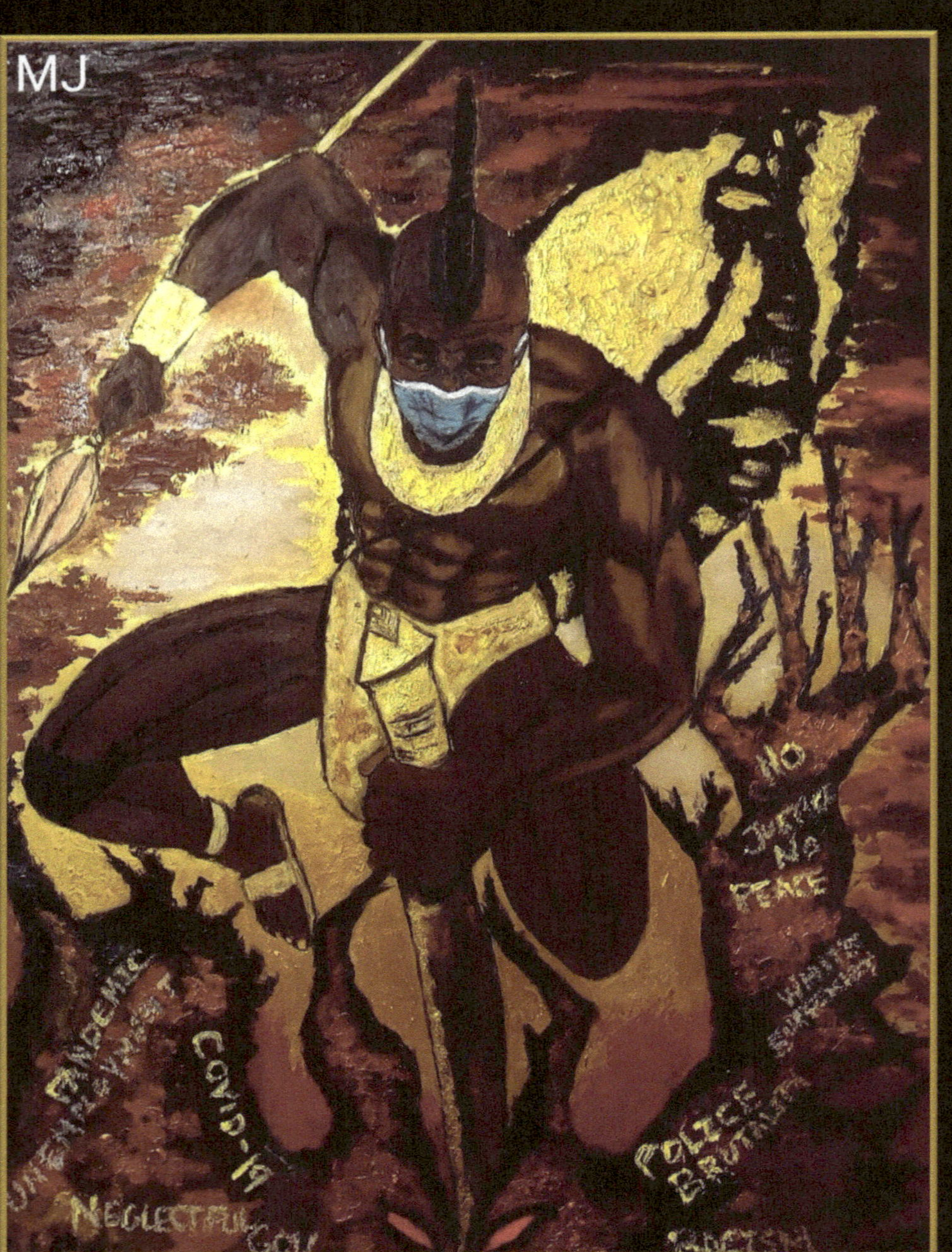

2020

Colored pencils, oil pastels, acrylic paint, and oil paint

2020 was a very challenging tumultuous year thanks to corvid and acts of injustice that tragically rocked the nation and the entire world, especially the deaths of George Floyd and Breonna Taylor at the police. Everyone dealt with 2020 in their own way. Some people protested others were forced to deal with themselves alone from the outside world. For others, 2020 forced people to fully tap deep within their talents which was my way of coping. In the painting, an African is shown attacking a demon that is the embodiment of all the bad things that occurred in 2020. It's a reminder of the integrity, resilience, and strength we showed through tragedy.

2021

Oil pastels, acrylic paint, and oil paint on wood canvas.

I follow and admire a well-known and respected artist on social media named Justin Wallington. On his Instagram page, I came across a photo of a lion whose left eye was wounded and related to him being blind in one eye. In early 2021, I went through an unsettling situation that later inspired me and decided to paint the wounded lion and name it, What Don't Kill Me Can Only Make Me Stronger. It has always been amazing to me how pain and danger can inspire someone to create the most fantastic work.

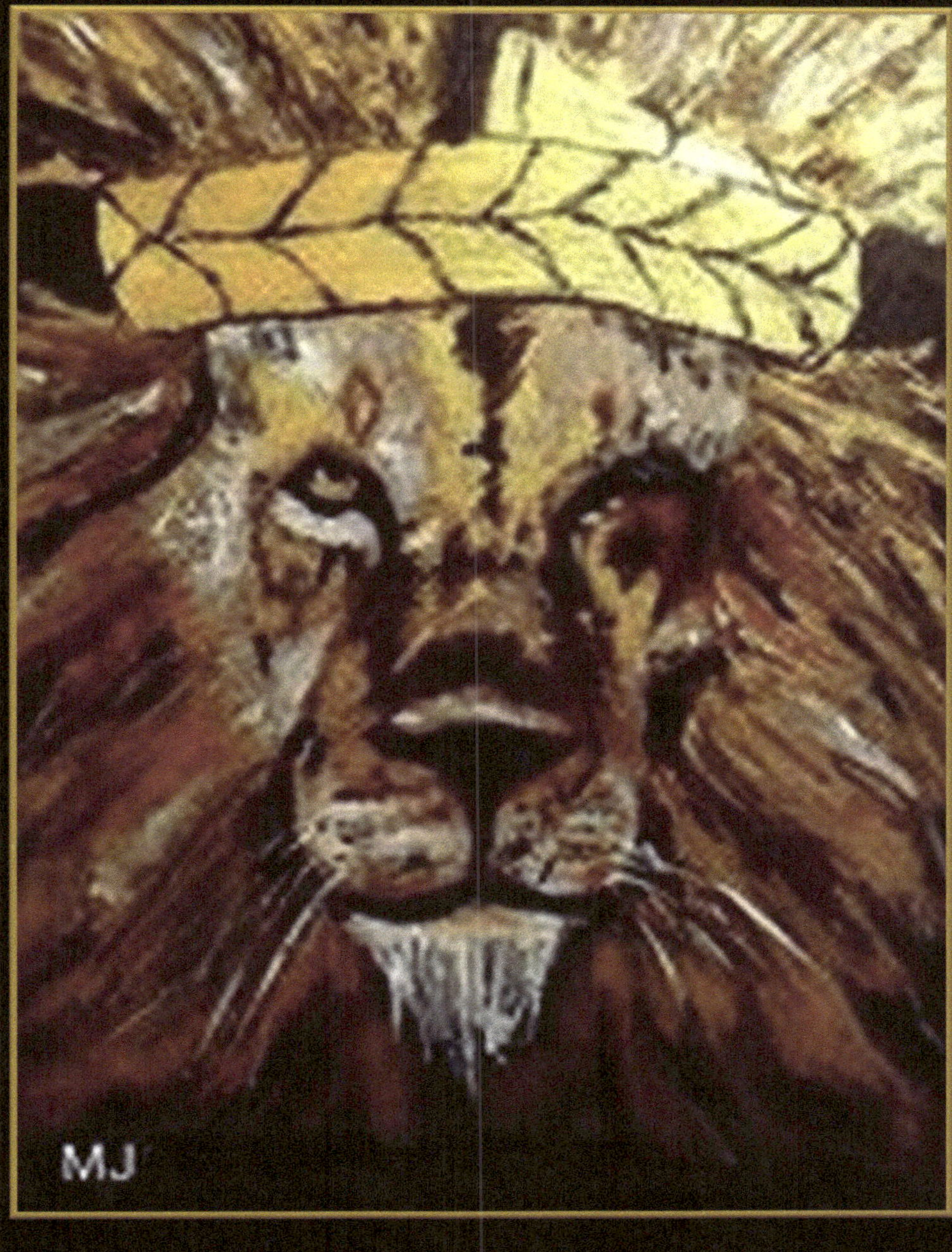

Nature In Winter series (1)

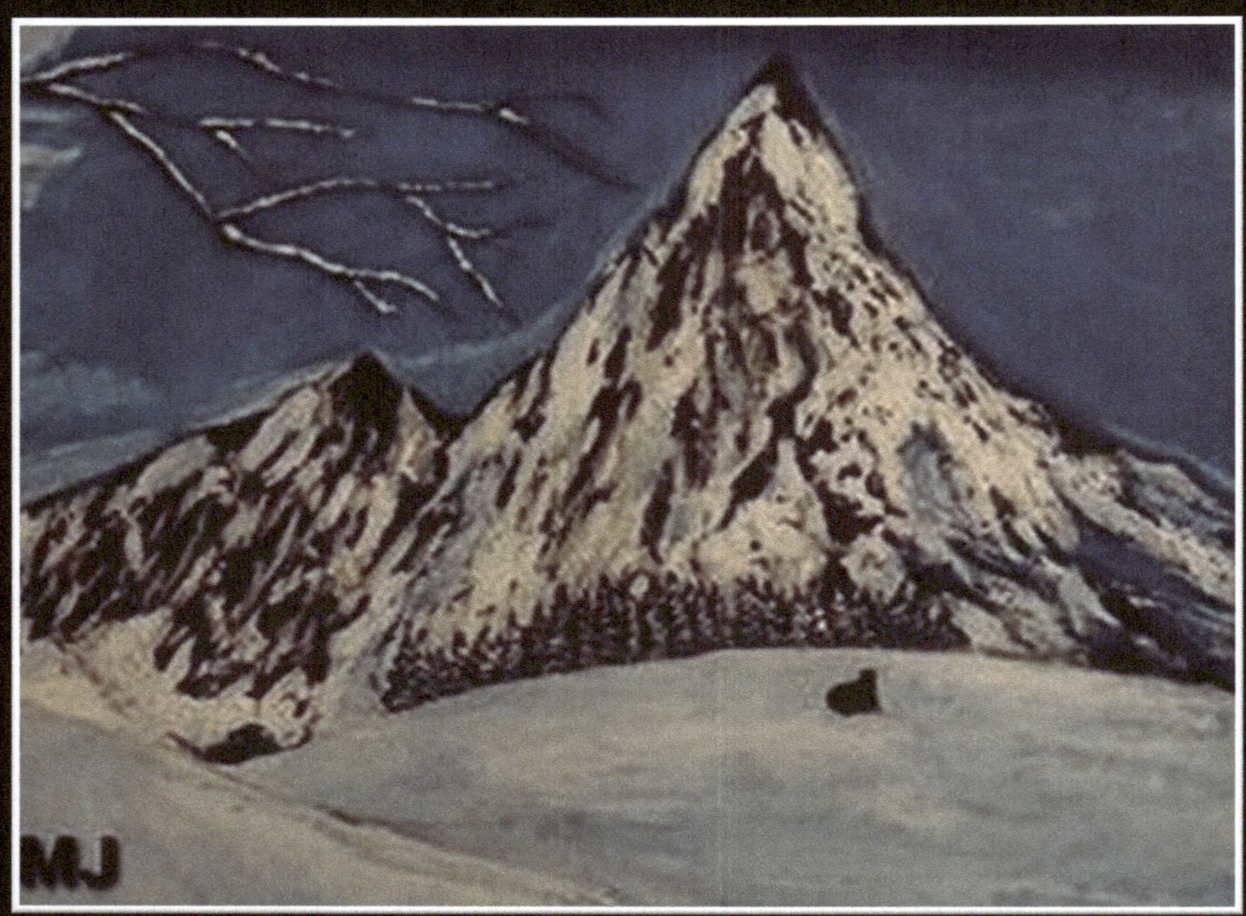

<u>2021</u>

Colored pencils, oil pastels, oil paint, and acrylic paint on wooden canvas.

I painted this series of three paintings dedicated to the season of Winter.

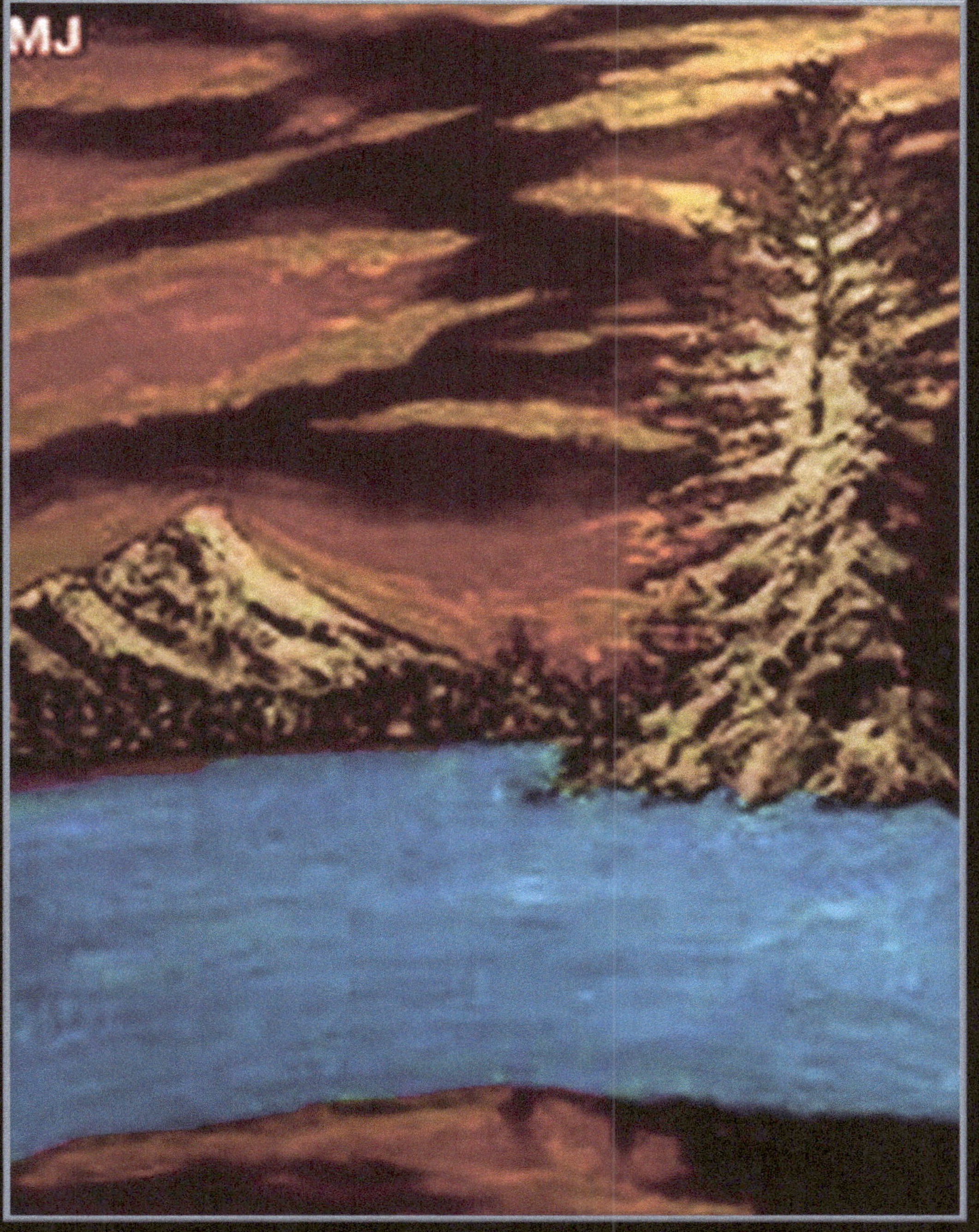

2021

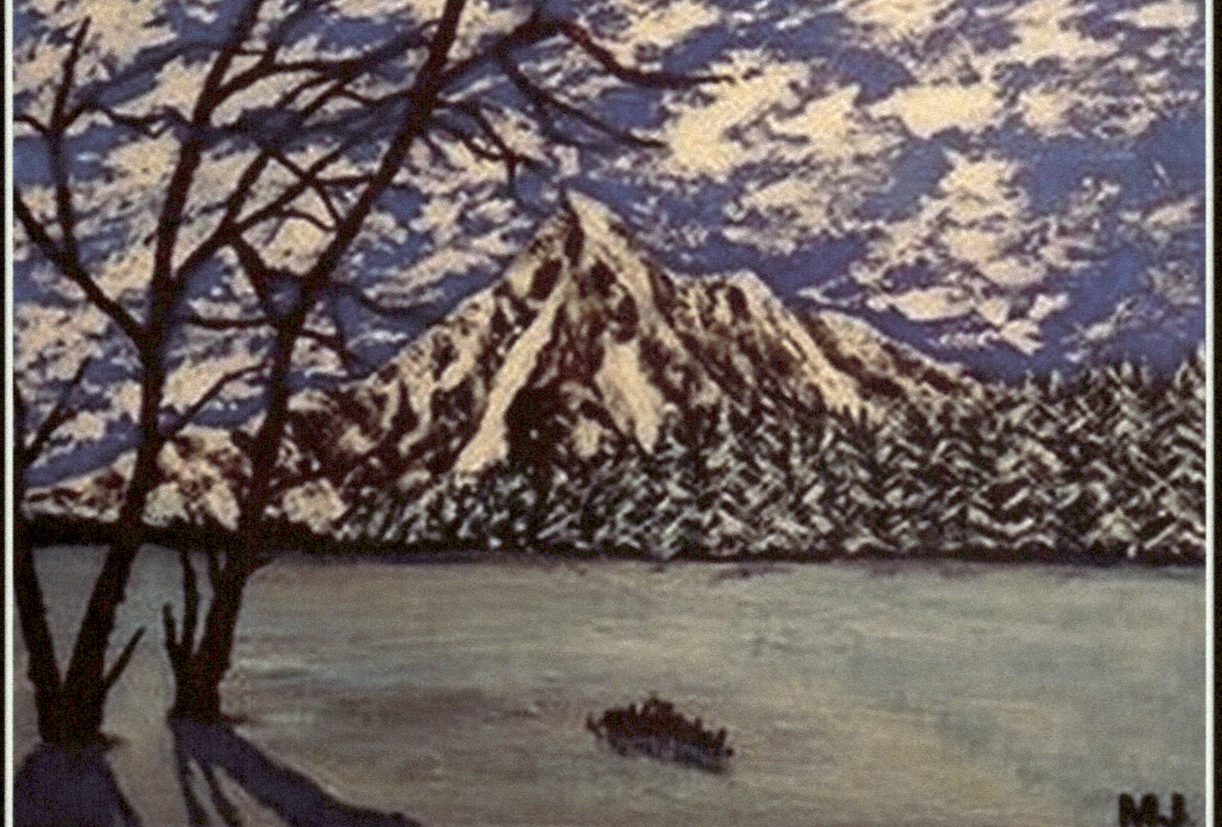

Your Love Is King

2021

Colored pencils, oil pastels, and acrylic paint on paper

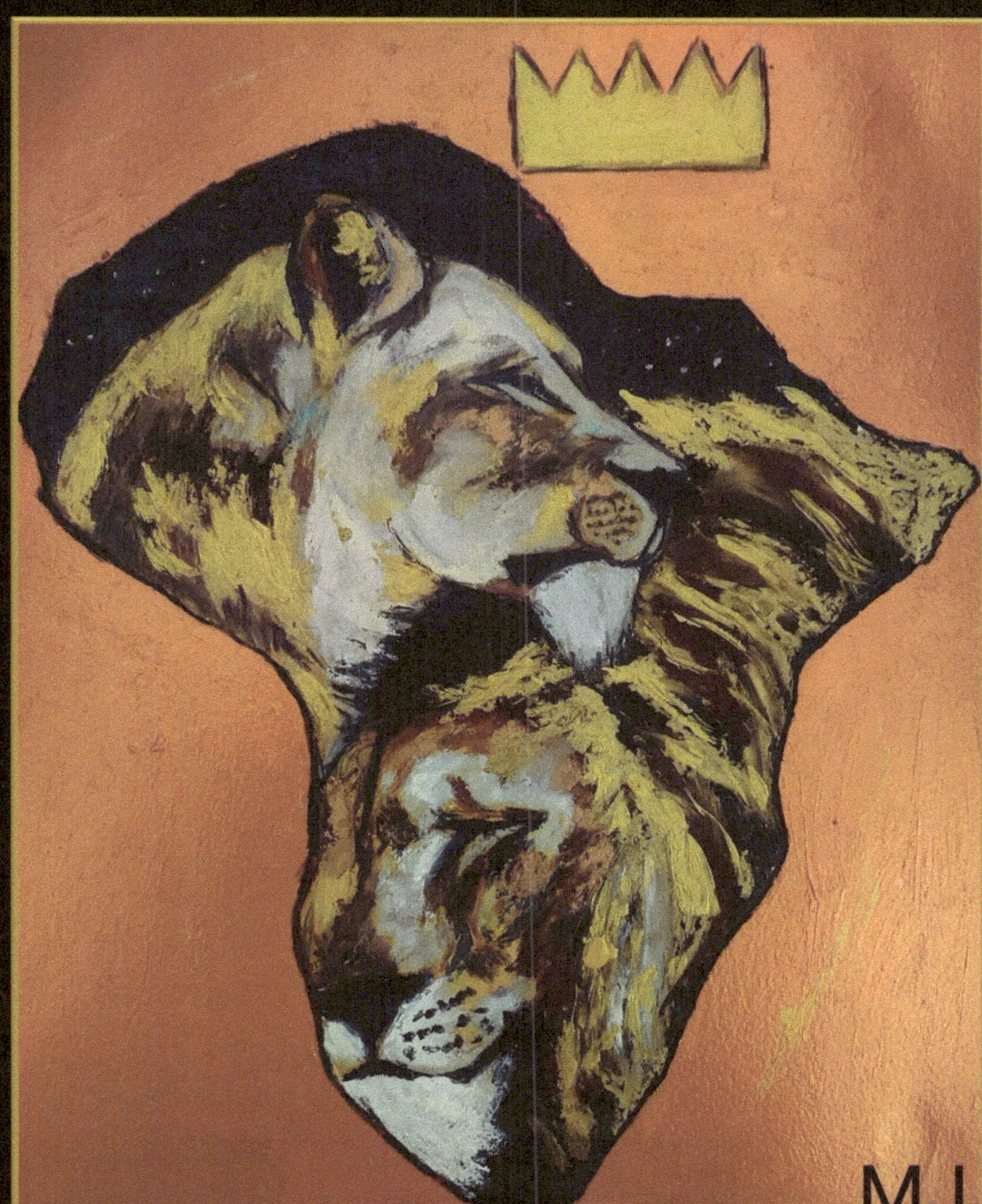

This portrait shows a male and female lion embraced and they're inside the continent of Africa.

Marvin Gaye Forever Eternal

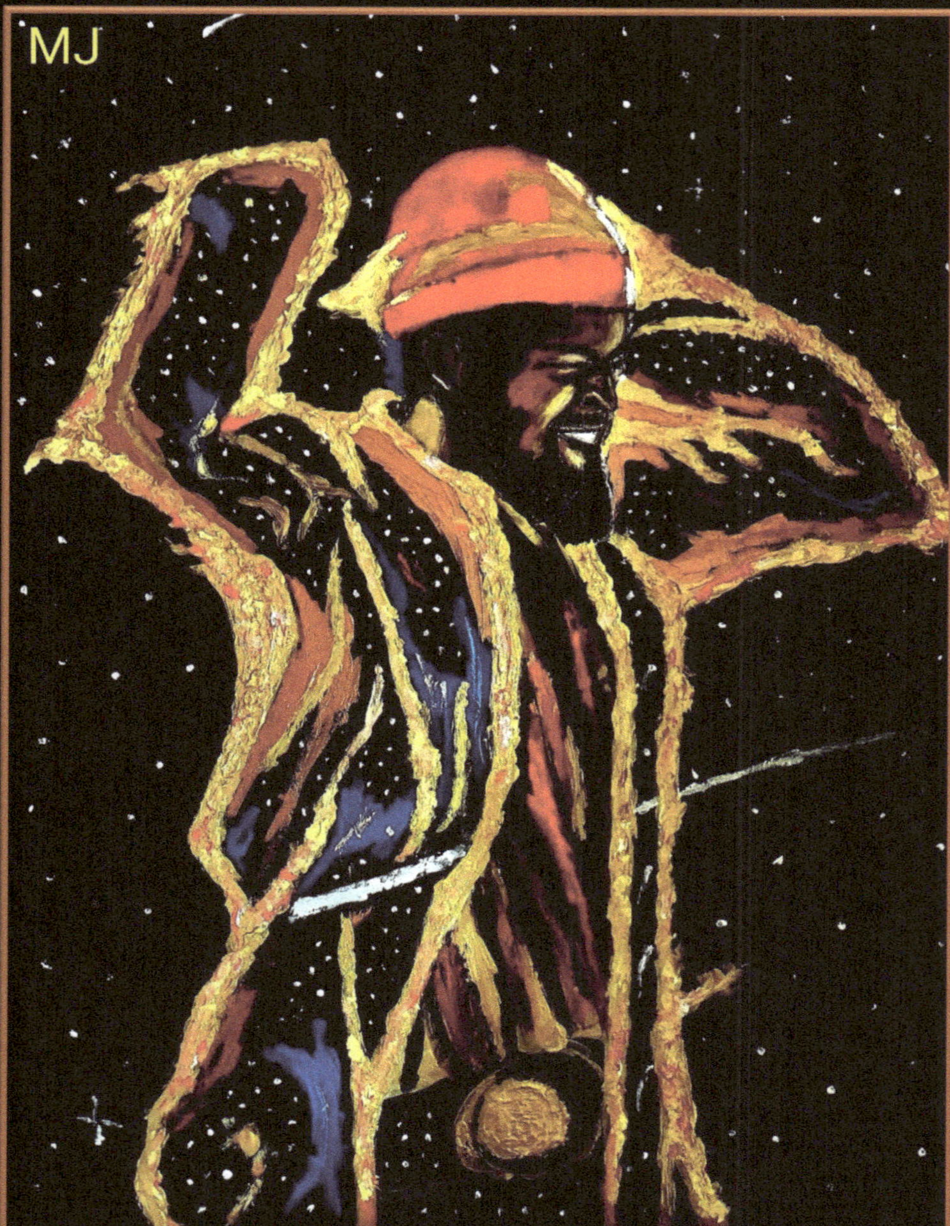

<u>*2021*</u>

Colored pencils, oil pastels, acrylic paint, and oil paint on wood canvas

Anyone who truly knows me, knows that I am a huge Marvin Gaye fan. His music, especially his What's Going On album, helped me through this crazy journey called life. In 2018, I created a portrait of him inspired by his What's Going on album cover. In April 2021, around the time of his birthday, I decided to paint another tribute dedicated to him, this time inspired by his Let's Get It On album cover.

Just like the portrait in 2018, I wanted to portray Marvin Gaye as a godly presence in the universe. His zodiac sign was fire, so I outlined his body in the appearance of fire. I would have to say that out of all the portraits I've done of Marvin Gaye, this one is my favorite.

MASTER J. HARRATTAN

Mothers Make the World Go Round

<u>*2021*</u>

Oil pastels, acrylic paint, and oil paint on canvas

I painted this beautiful piece in the month of May around the time of Mother's Day, which makes this painting very special to me. During the process, I thought about my mother, the major sacrifices she's made, and how hard she worked to provide for me and my sister. Also, I thought about the wisdom she's passed down to me and to many other youths as a schoolteacher. Mothers are the first teachers. They are the ones who usually provide wisdom, along with nurturing, which helps mold us into the human beings that we become. That is why I gave this painting the title, Mother's Make the World Go Round. I painted a black woman holding the earth within her womb, she is glowing and is the universe. I wanted to display her as a goddess.

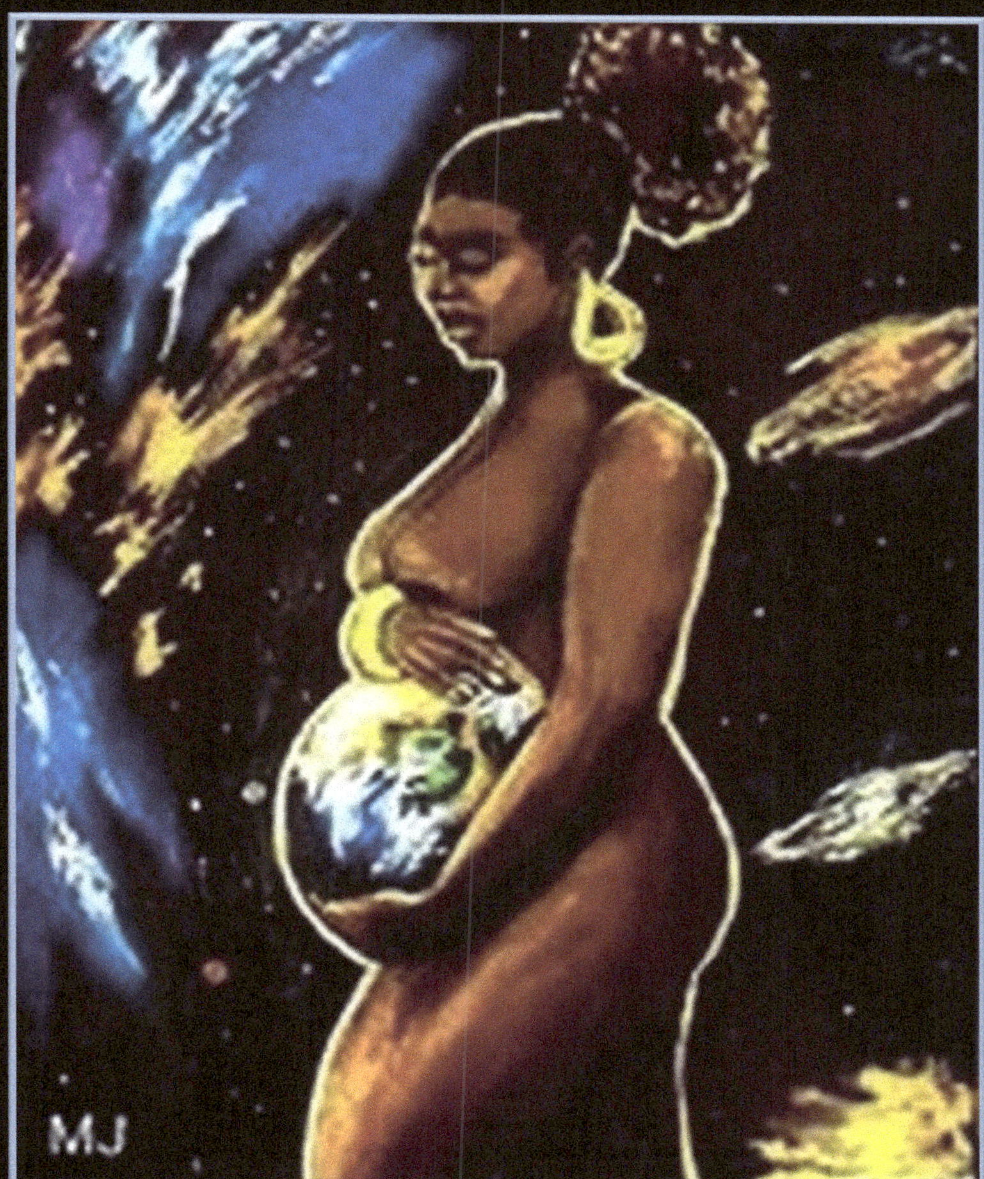

Above the Clouds (Portrait of Kobe Bryant)

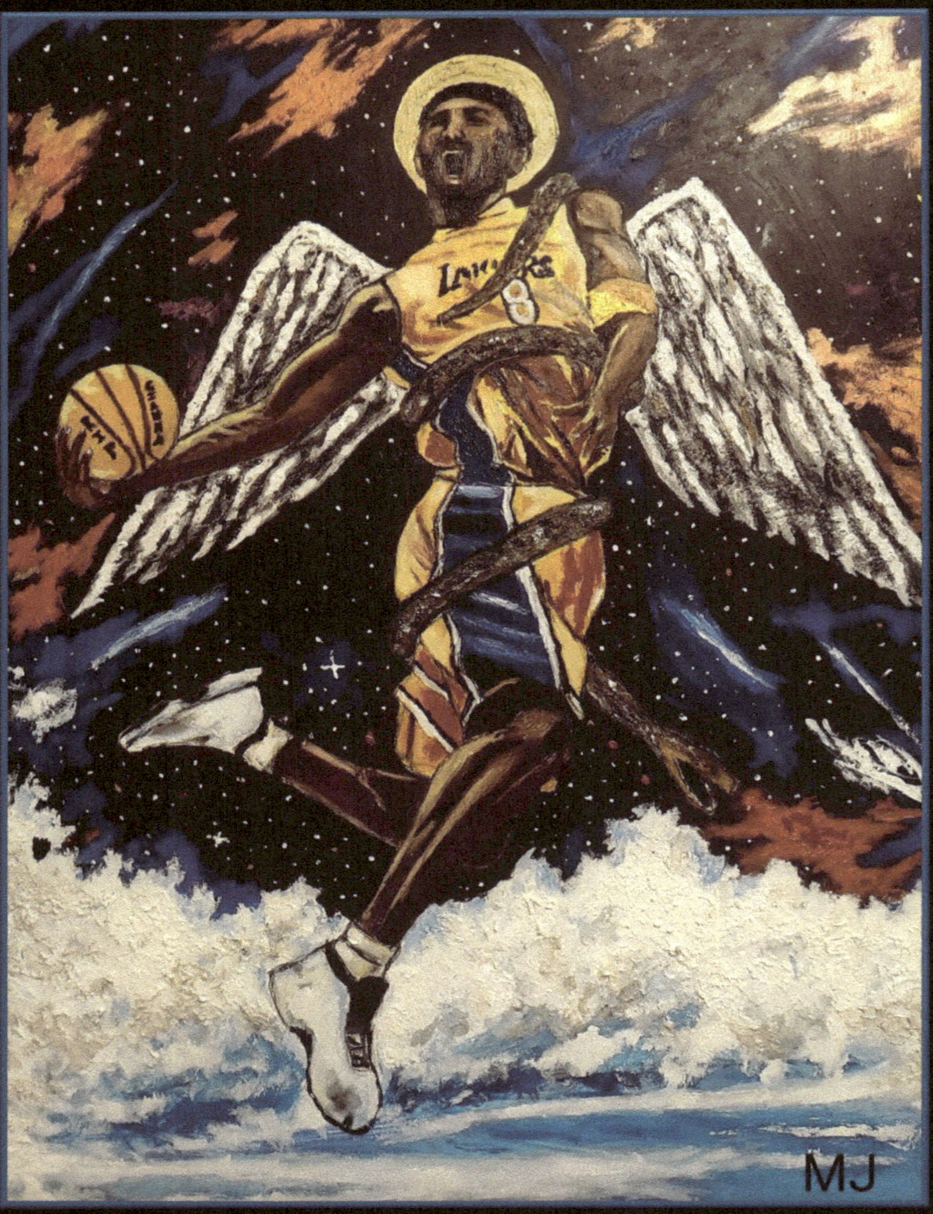

<u>2021</u>

Colored pencils, oil pastels, acrylic paint, and oil paint on wooden canvas

This is another painting that I feel is some of my greatest work. I waited a full year to paint Kobe Bryant, but during the wait, I already envisioned how I wanted to portray him. I titled the portrait, Above the Clouds, because it shows Kobe ascending over clouds and coming into the universe with angel wings. I made sure that I acknowledged his daughter by painting her name, Gianna, on his basketball. As we all know, she passed away along with Kobe.

Kobe Bryant was an incredible athlete. He had ambition and drive like no other on the court. He was also big on encouraging others to be their selves. He will never be forgotten.

The Fighter

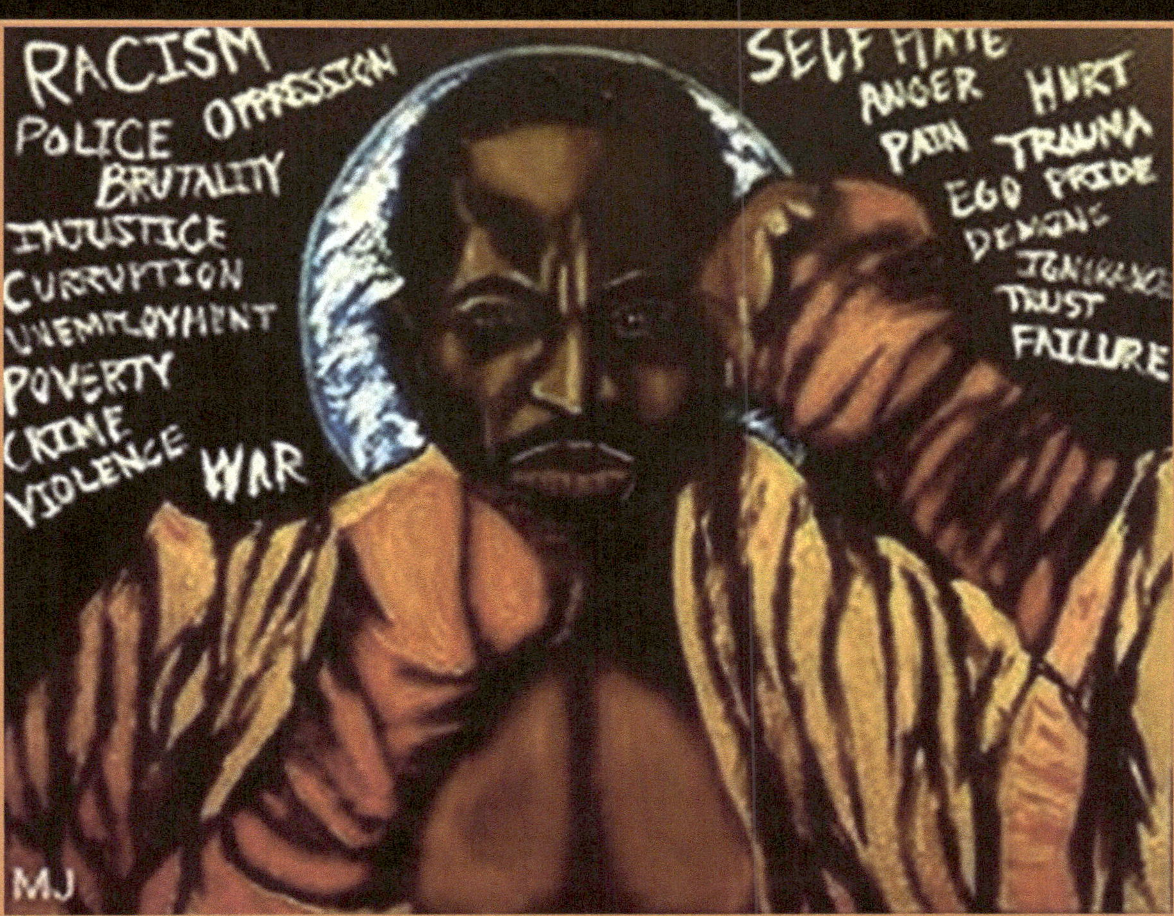

<u>2021</u>

Colored pencils, oil pastels, acrylic paint, and oil paint on canvas

This painting is very special to me and is one of my favorite pieces of art. It gives a very important message that anyone can relate to. I gave this painting the title, The Fighter, because I believe that everyone has a fighting spirit within that keeps them going and pushing forward. I painted a black man because I and so many black men can relate to this painting. We have been fighting to survive and exist for ions. I painted the world behind the man to symbolize the mentality that a lot have thinking the world is against us. The black man is dressed in a boxer robe and his fists are wrapped up to symbolize the fighter. He is surrounded by issues that we as black men have dealt with daily.

Til Shiloh (Portrait of Buju Banton)

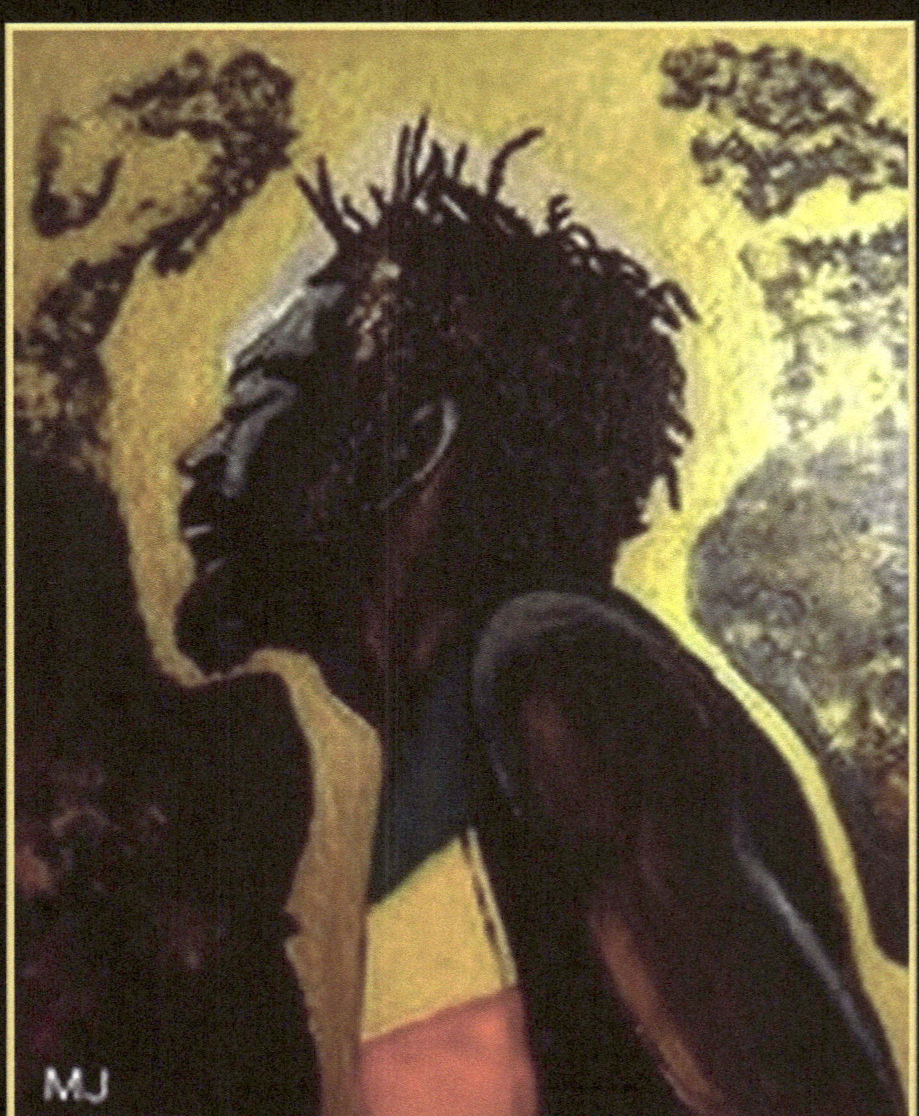

<u>*2021*</u>

Oil pastels, acrylic paint, and oil paint on wood canvas

I grew up listening to dance hall reggae. As a teenager I remember owning only two reggae albums, one of them was Til Shilosh from Jamaican reggae artist, Buju Banton. I remember owning the cassette tape and would play it back-to-back. The tape went through hell, but thankfully was still able to play.

In early 2021 I painted this tribute of Buju after learning that it was the anniversary of the album. This is a painting of the album cover of Til Shiloh.

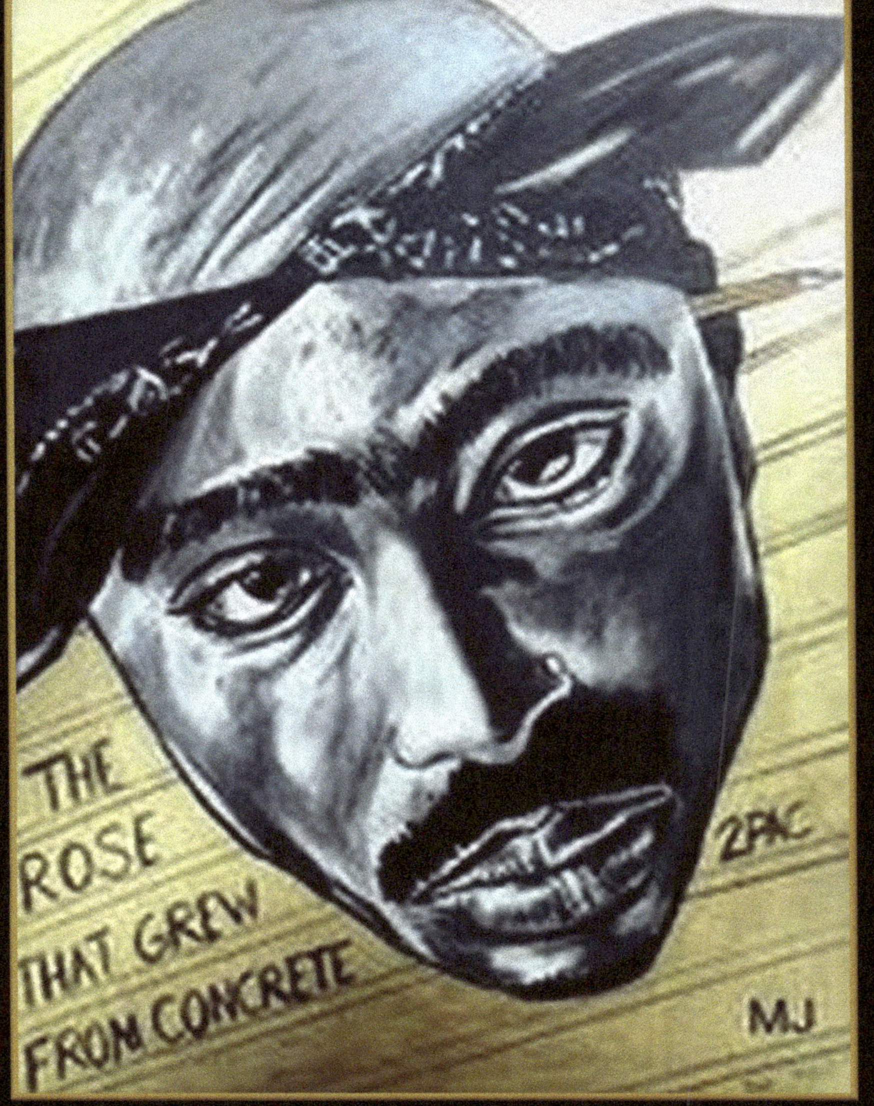

<u>2021</u>

Graphite pencils, colored pencils, oil paint marker and acrylic paint on paper.

Tupac Shakur I would say is my all-time favorite hip-hop artist. He was wise beyond his years. The way Tupac used his words immediately reeled you in, and you could feel what he was talking about even if you couldn't relate to it. He was definitely blessed with the gift of speech.

While I was creating this portrait, I thought about a collection of poetry that Tupac wrote before he became a rap artist called, A Rose That Grew from Concrete. My goal was to make Pac appear as writing paper.

Royalty (KING)

2021

Colored pencils, oil pastels, oil paint, and acrylic paint on wood canvas

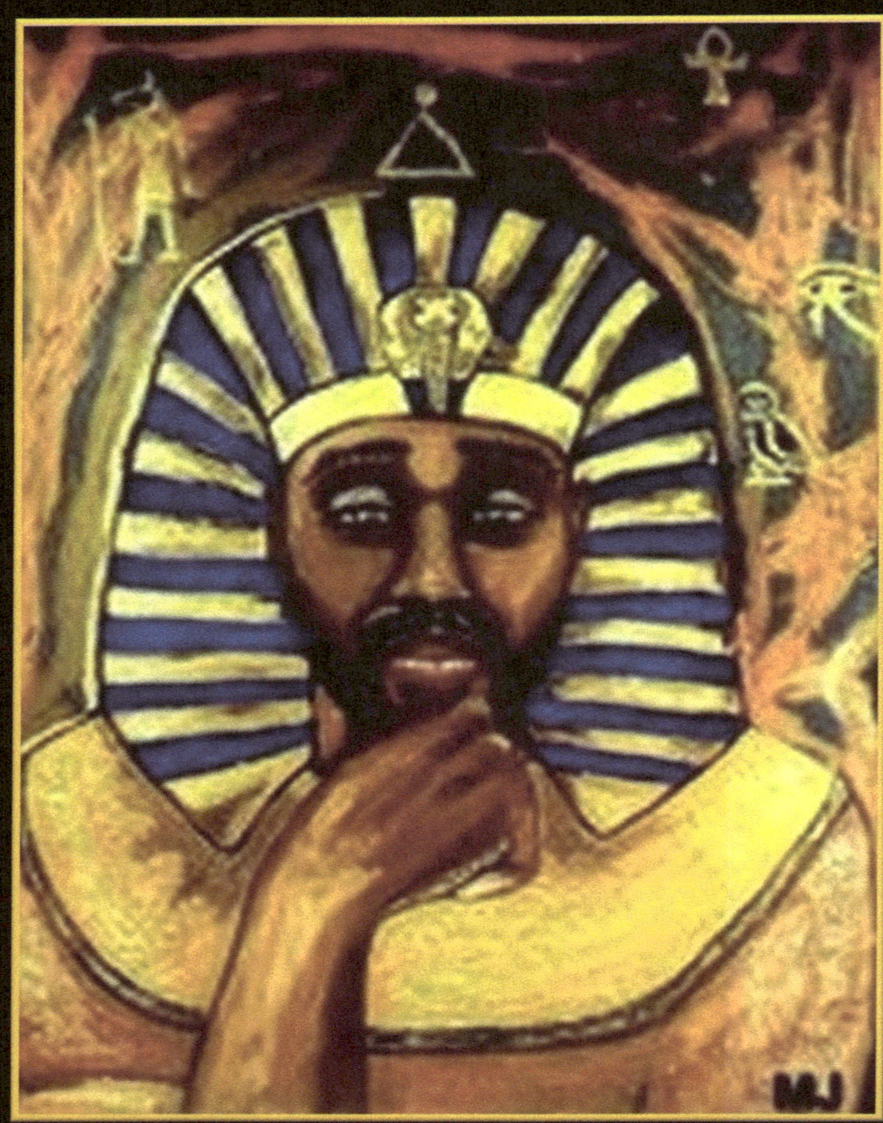

I feel that it is very important we as black people think highly and positive of ourselves. It is a must since overall society still refuses to recognize our full worth. This painting is very special to me because it expresses how I feel about myself currently. It was done on my birthday, and I wanted to display a black man as the most positive yet powerful way possible, as a king. I painted him as a Pharaoh and titled it, Royalty (King).

Elegant Woman/ Beautiful Queen

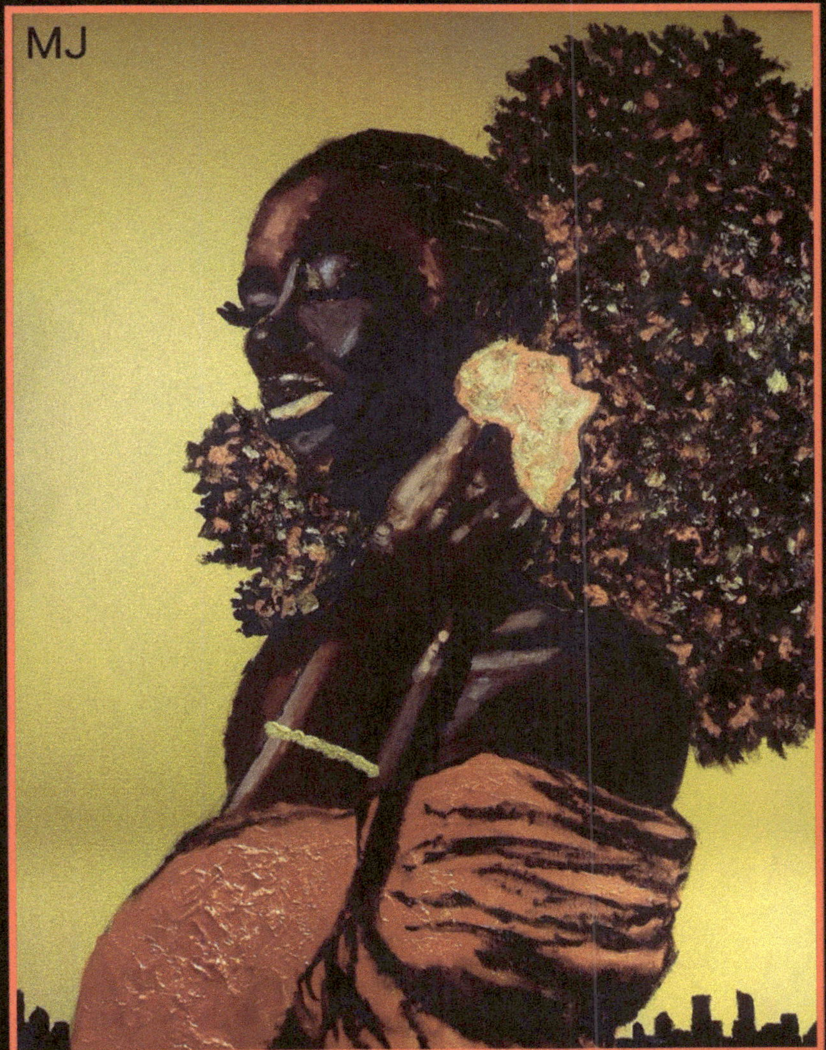

2021

Oil paint, acrylic paint, oil pastels, and colored pencil on gold canvas.

One day after work I came to an art store. While there I found a stack of 16x20 gold canvases and being that I love the color gold, I bought one. On my way back to the train, I immediately knew what I wanted to paint on the canvas. The painting shows a black woman in a moment of elegance. When it came to her hair, I added clumps of oil pastel and acrylic paint to create texture.

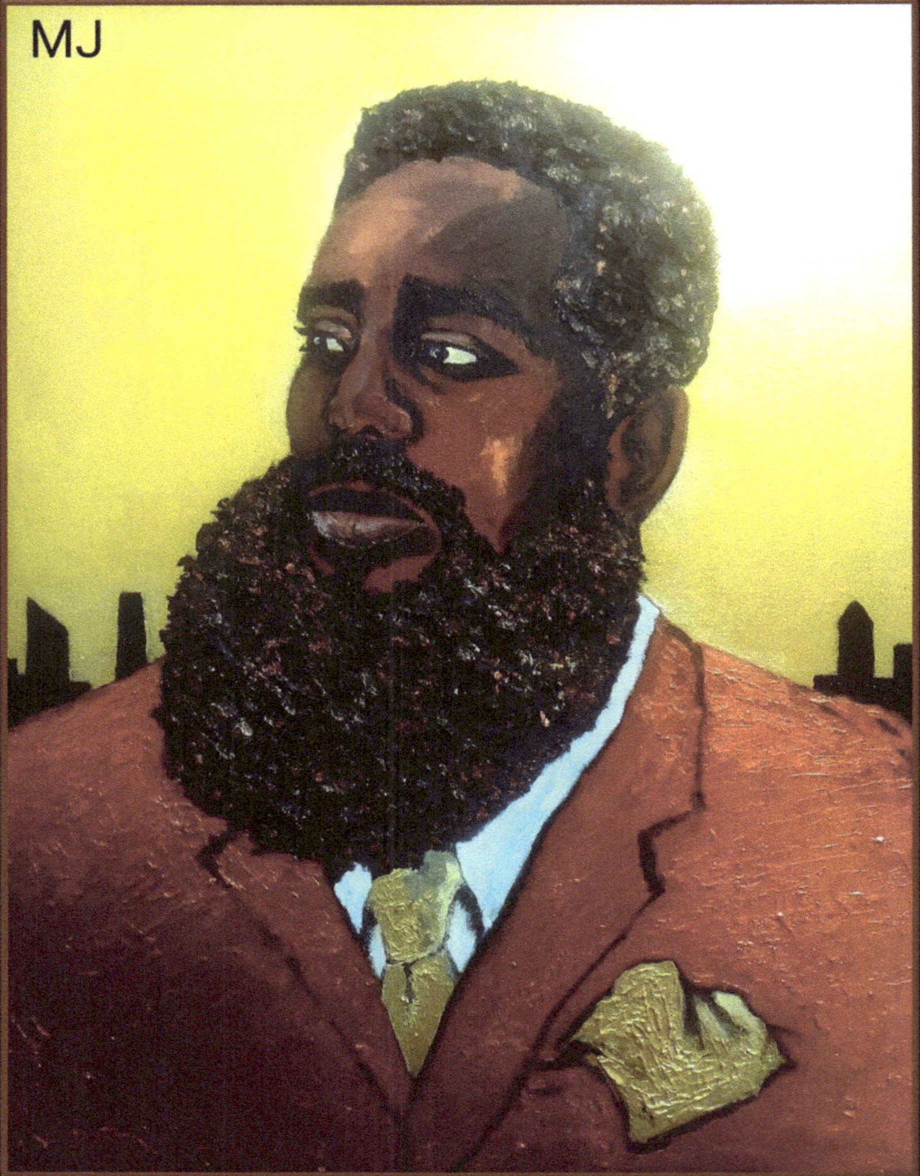

This painting means a lot to me because it is a reminder that I am a living success. when creating this piece, I thought about every black man that has beaten any odds that were thrown against him in life.

Like Elegant Woman (Black Queen), I added clumps of oil pastels and acrylic paint to his beard to create texture.

Sunset Over The Waters

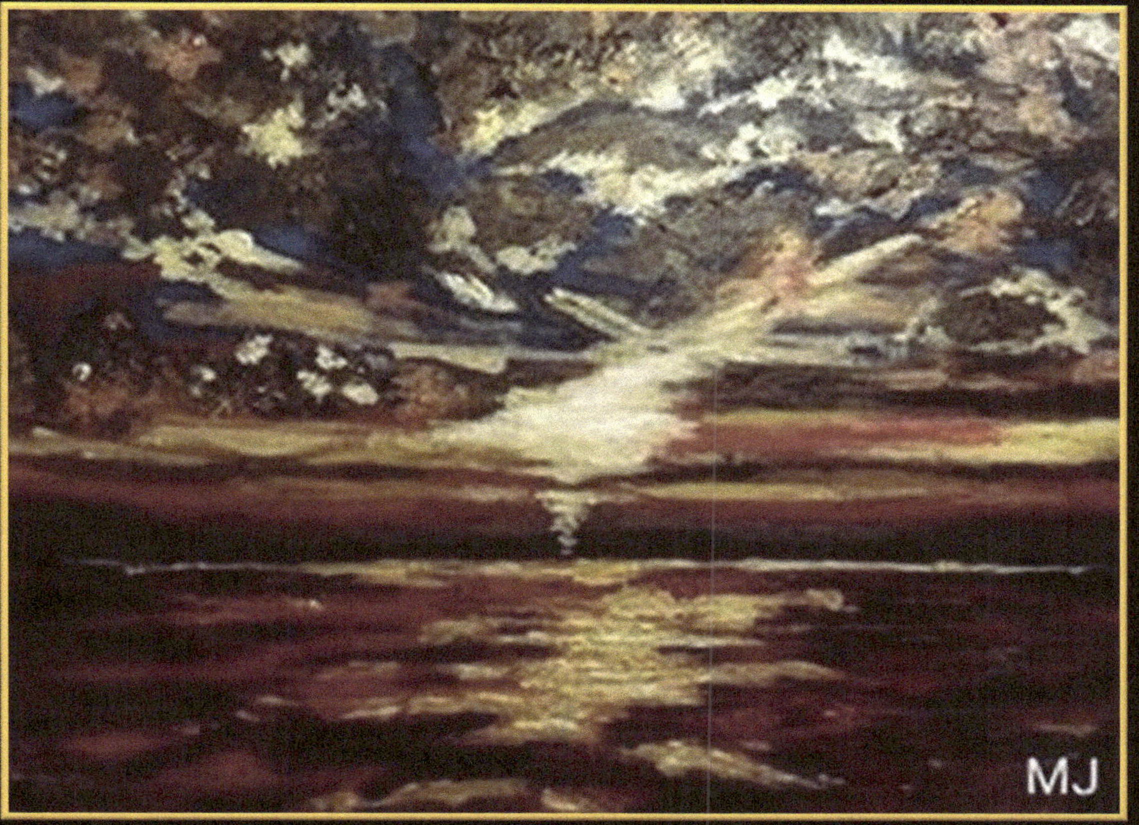

<u>2021</u>

Oil paint and acrylic paint on canvas

I love sunsets. I find them to be one of the most beautiful moments of nature to experience, especially sunsets over water.

Full Golden Moon

2021

*Oil paint and acrylic paint
on canvas*

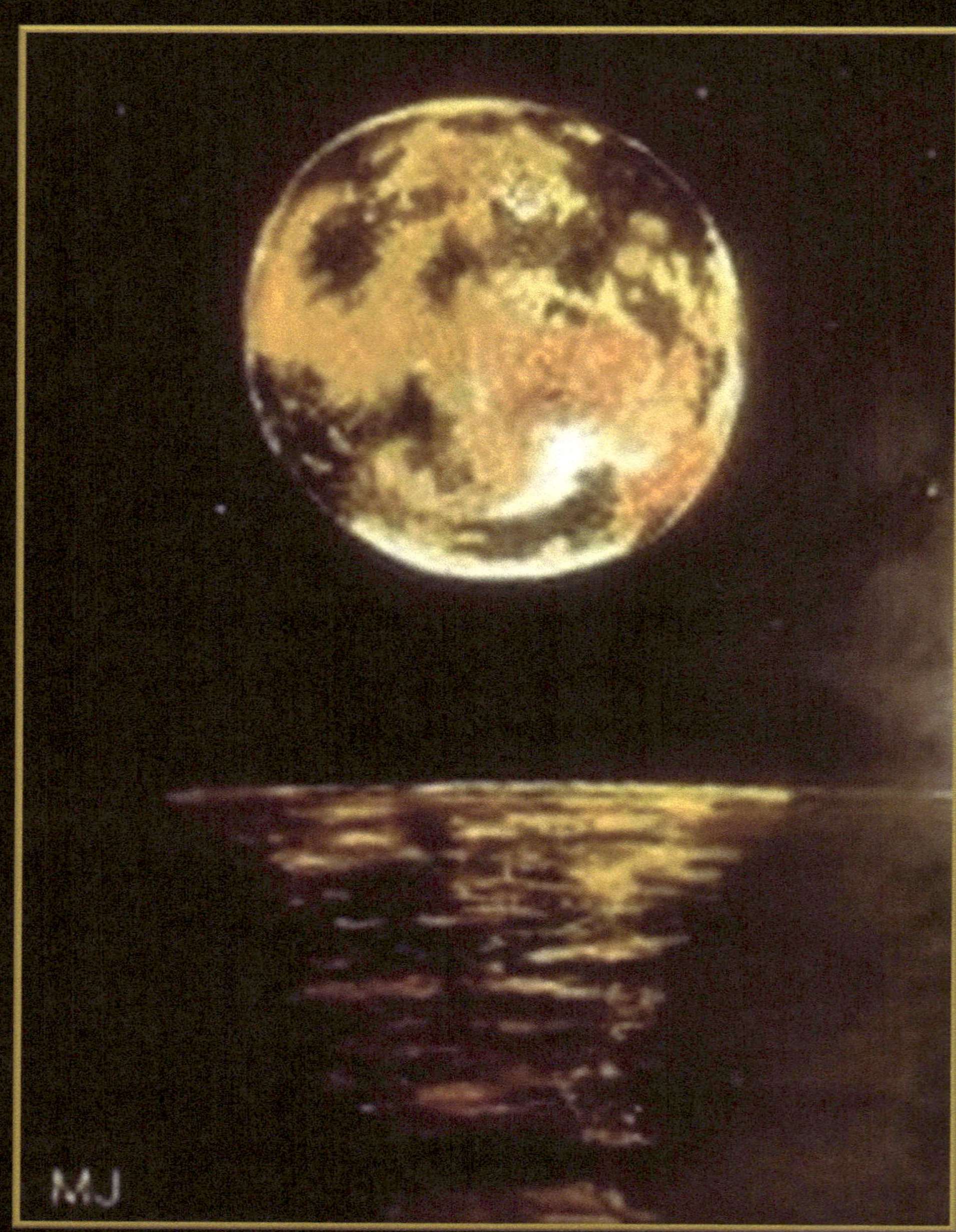

As an artist, I have realized that sometimes an idea won't always turn out successful and you must start from scratch. In this case, the canvas was originally going to be used to create a portrait of DMX, but it wasn't coming out right, which frustrated me a little but after much thought, I decided to create a night scene of golden full moon with its reflection on the ocean water.

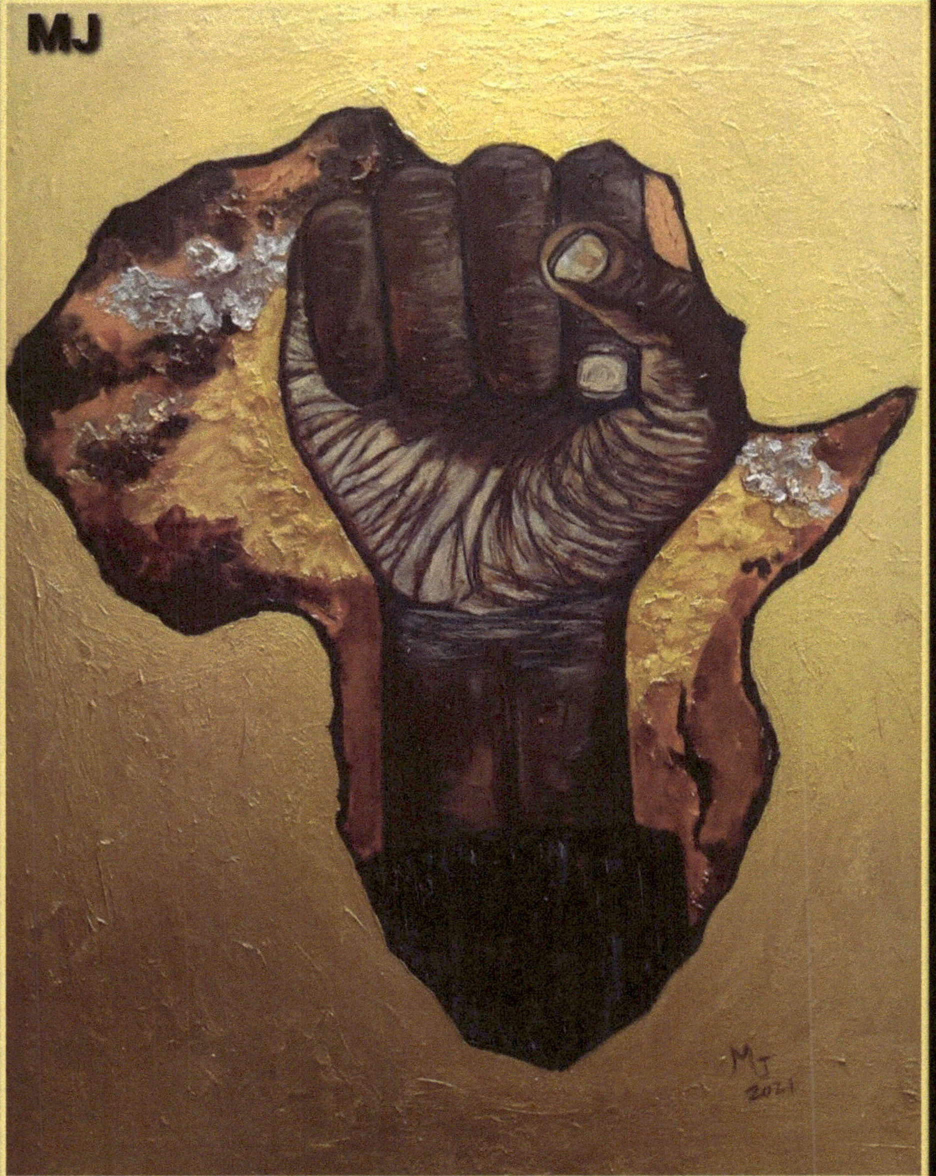

Colored pencils, oil pastels, and acrylic paint on wood canvas

In this painting titled, My Roots, I wanted to pay homage to my ancestral roots and to show pure pride of who I am and where my roots are. I used my own hand made into a fist and drew and painted it inside the continent of Africa. I painted the water gold because gold is a powerful color that defines royalty and importance.

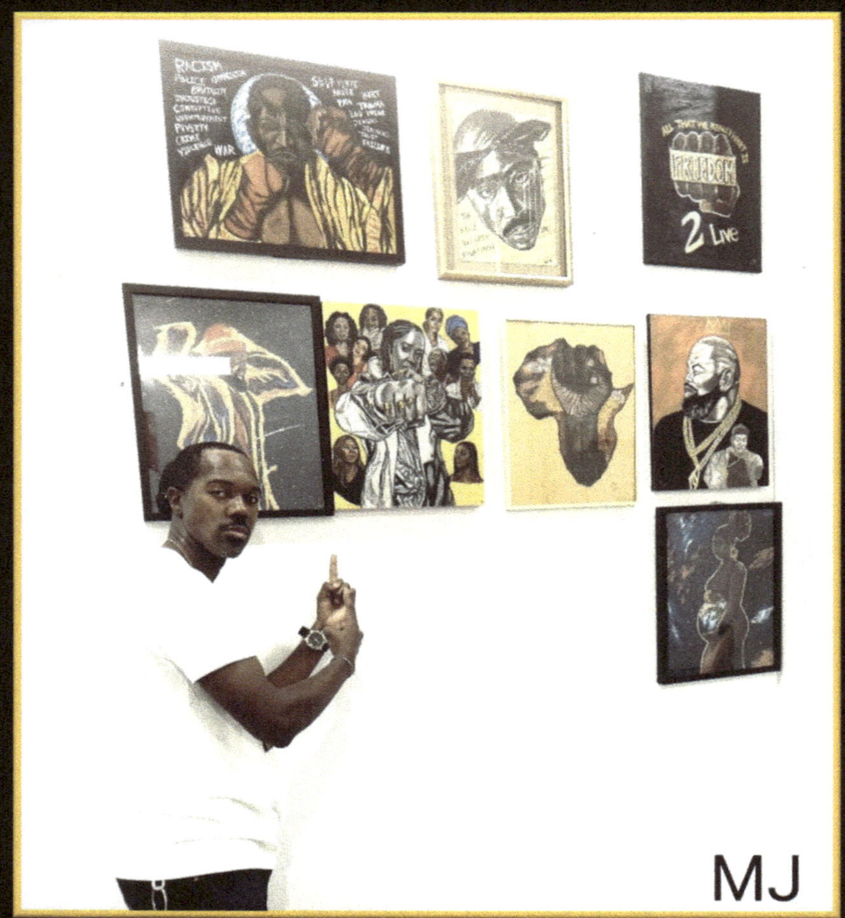

I was born and raised in New York, NY, and art has always been a huge part of my life - ever since I was a little boy. One particular memory that will forever stay within my mind is when my mother told me a story about when I was hyper as a little child, she placed a crayon and a piece of paper before me to draw and it calmed me down. From then on, I never stopped creating.

Through my journey as an artist, I drew inspiration from watching painter, Bob Ross. I was amazed at how he was able to create scenes of nature out of his imagination within 30 minutes. I too then started drawing mainly outdoor scenes of nature from my imagination. Later, I started painting and drawing portraits of people and animals and learning about themes and concepts in art while being a student at Pratt Institute Art School (which deeply humbled me).

I have been blessed with the opportunity to show my art on gallery walls at *One Art Space Gallery* in Tribeca, Manhattan, NY, galleries in Brooklyn, and most recently, showing my art in a mansion. My next goal as an artist is to become an entrepreneur. Art has been many things for me but it has mainly been my instrument for expressing my deepest thoughts and feelings that words cannot describe plus also expressing my deep love for my culture. Art has become therapy for me, my true savior from my darkest times in life. Everything is art. If anything can be created from scratch, it is art, and I'm glad that I was born with the gift to create.